The Bhagavad Gita

The Bhagavad Gita

A Transcreation of The Song Celestial

ALAN JACOBS

BOOKS

Winchester, UK
New York, USA

*Dedicated to
all my fellow men and women
who are seeking Truth*

About the author

Alan Jacobs is a retired art dealer. He is now the Chair
of the Ramana Maharshi Foundation UK.
He is editor and compiler of:

Poetry for the Spirit, Watkins Publishing 2001, formerly
The Element Book of Mystical Verse, Element Books, 1997.

Reflections: An Anthology of Contemporary Mystic Verse,
Rowan Press 2000.

His poetry is published regularly in the magazines
Reflections and *Self Enquiry* and in the collection *The
Pearl Fishers,* published by the Broadfield Press, 1997.

Jacobs commenced his search in 1957 and since then has
made an extensive inquiry into the teachings of George
Gurdjieff, Jiddu Krishnamurti, Jean Klein, Ramana
Maharshi, Douglas Harding, and
Ramesh Balsekar.

Contents

APPENDICES

Invocation

Obeisance unto That,
The underlying form of
Everything,
In which is everything,
From which everything
Emerges.

Which is everything,
Is everywhere
Is that Reality – Consciousness –
Peace,
The Underlying form of
Everything.

From Mahabharata Shanti Parva 46

Preface

The book of milk and honey

This epic Mahabharata
Is a bright blue water lily.
Her Gita is the precious pollen;
Sipping as a humble bumble bee,
Relish her sweet nectar
And bathe yourself in her
Honey of wisdom

The Mystic Doctrine
Of the Upanishads
Are the Sacred Cows,
The symbols of Brahman-Atman

Lord Krishna was the divine
Milkman,
Arjuna was his beloved calf,
And the good nourishment
Is the Bhagavad Gita,
The sweet cream of Krishna's milking.

Foreword

Why this Gita is different from any other Gitas

There have been countless translations of the Bhagavad Gita, this beautiful Song of God has captured the hearts and minds of every generation for over 2500 years.

This book is not a translation, rather it is a "transcreation". The archaic text of previous scholarly translations has been enlivened by the use of contemporary free verse, expansion of metaphors and most importantly an advaitic or non-dual approach to the text, which differs radically from traditional literal translations of the past.

The great Shankara in his seminal commentary on the Gita made it expressively clear that in the Bhagavad Gita we have the higher, para vidya, or esoteric, absolute, non dual, advaitic teaching interwoven with the lower, apara vidya or exoteric, relative, dualistic traditional teaching. This was for those un-initiated into the Brahmanic esoteric circle, who were pointed to Self-Realization under the direct guidance of a guru.

Thanks to the great gift of Grace culminating in Bhagavan Ramana Maharshi's advent on our planet in this dark era of the Kali Yuga, the esoteric meaning can now be made accessible to all, as with his important Atma Vichara of Self Inquiry.

It is now an "open secret" for those receptive enough to appreciate it, and in the transcreation and brief commentary

I have endeavored to highlight and pinpoint this distinction and avoid the confusion of the para vidya and apara vidya being read side by side, by the reader who lacks this knowledge.

This magnificent scripture has been placed as an episode in the Mahabharata, the great epic of ancient India. The Mahabharata, like Homer's *Odyssey*, transmits the wisdom and spirit of the Vedic Civilization, a high point of culture on our planet, from where spiritual inspiration first sprang and spread throughout the ancient world.

It is as if the sages knew that to spread the Eternal Message of the Gita they must place it in the center of a popular book like the Mahabharata, which was widely read and enjoyed by the masses.

Its date, according to the universally accepted authority, Prof. S. Radhakrishnan, may be safely assigned to the fifth century BCE. The authorship is attributed to the sage Vyasa, the legendary compiler of the Mahabharata. It is possibly almost an exact rendition of the words Lord Krishna recited on the battlefield to Arjuna. It is an inspired revelation, a perennial message to humanity, the foundation of the Hindu religion, and a wonderful gift to us all to alleviate the suffering and confusion of our perplexed humanity.

As Shankara writes in the introduction to his commentary, "the subject is the Para-Brahman, the object is Salvation, Moksha."[1] This book is primarily intended for those who seek deliverance from the turmoil of Samsara.[2] I have endeavored through Sri Bhagavan Ramana Maharshi's Grace to follow this tradition.

Alan Jacobs
May 2003

---

[1] Self-Realization
[2] World illusion

Introduction

There are now 279 translations[1] of the Bhagavad Gita into the English language since Warren Hastings, the far-sighted Governor of the East Indian Company, revealed this magnificent book to the West. It is a sacred scripture of epic dimension and is the gospel of Hinduism. Literally, Bhagavad Gita means the "Song of God" and it is often called the "Song Celestial." Mahatma Gandhi lived his life by the Gita and was then able to liberate India from British Colonial rule. Every translation is different and has its own unique approach, angularity, delineation and emphasis.

The archaic English translations needed dusting down. This is a transcreation and the text has been expanded to reinforce the poetic imagery and power. It is, therefore, not a literal translation, which always suffer through the process. It is "juicy" rather than arid and occasionally "over the top." Originally, the Gita was written as poetry, as are all Indian scriptures, and never as prose. So much is lost when the poetry is translated into prose. The fine poetic translation by

[1] Researched in the British Library.
The Bhagavad Gita had been published in 75 languages and in each language there have been several publications. According to the statistics there are 70 publications of the Gita in Tamil, 150 in Telugu, 132 in Marathi, 384 in Bengali, 25 in French, 28 in German and 279 in English. Now there are several more translations and commentaries on the Gita. According to one estimate there are about 2000 translations and commentaries in various languages of the world today, no one interpreting it in exactly the same way as another.

the English poet, Sir Edwin Arnold, was completed in 1855 and has never been out of print. Indian school children still learn it by heart, even today. The Spanish Poet Juan Mascaro, who has also made a very praiseworthy prose-poetry translation, wrote that the Arnold translation will always be the most popular. Unfortunately, the Arnold translation has now become archaic and versified in the heroic meter of Shakespeare's iambic pentameters. It is not as "instantaneous" or easily read as our contemporary free verse, amenable for today's reader. I have reduced the number of Sanskrit words by giving them their best English translation in the text. I have also kept Krishna's name as Krishna rather than use many alternatives, which can confuse the dialogue.

The Gita is a sacred text and must be read with due caution. It is a transforming instrument. It commences with a plea for spiritual practice as an opening step and then moves into the wider perspective of the mystical vision of the One, the Self, the Witnessing Consciousness. It is a step-by-step process and each verse leads to the next. One must read the whole. Chapter I sets the scene, Chapter II the agenda and Chapter XVIII the solution. But do not skip the beautiful verses in between; it is like a great symphony. Each chapter relates to the last but leads on to the coda.

As my late teacher, Kenneth Walker, wrote in his autobiography, *I talk of Dreams*:

> The battlefield of Kurashetra is the battlefield of one's own life; Arjuna, Krishna, Dhritarashva, Sanjaya, etc represent different sides of one's being.
>
> Dhritrashva means "the man who has seized the kingdom" and it stands for the empirical ego in us. (He is blind.)
>
> Krishna represents the higher or more God-like qualities in us.
>
> Arjuna is that part of a man which sees the warring elements

within him; but, although he sees them doesn't want to commit himself too much by taking sides.

This is therefore a popular transcreation, largely with the Western reader in mind, not a scholarly translation, using contemporary free verse based on "innovative metaphors" and figures of speech and swift line breaks. W. B. Yeats, the great Irish poet, also translated the Gita in conjunction with a Sanskrit scholar, as did the novelist Christopher Isherwood. Both of these important writers concentrated on clear meaning rather than poetic resonance. The true meaning has also been greatly obscured by nineteenth-century pseudo-biblical translations, which imitate Old Testament cadence to the detriment of the text and its essential meaning. I hope to convey the poetry and still adhere to the true meaning. It is mandala poetry – each verse is a mandala for meditation.

So as to assist readers to understand the word Self, confused by our dualistic language, I repeat it often by synonyms such as:

Absolute Consciousness
Grace
Awareness
Love
Truth
Peace
Bliss
Space
Godhead

The word Self in English is obscure and often ambiguous. People think it refers to their individuality. In fact it is That in which individuality appears. God is often referred to as He. It could be She or He *and* She. But I have mainly kept to the convention of He. The Gita advises "him" it also implies "her." I have kept to "him." Her is implied. According to Professor Radhakrishnan whose philosophic rather than poetic translation of the Gita I would recommend to those of intellectual bent, the Gita dates to the fifth century BCE. It is a compilation of Sankhya philosophy, and Upanishadic teaching. It is indeed possible that Krishna, the historical king referred to in the Upanishadis, was the compiler. Vyasa is the legendary author. The Gita comes from another culture; now, 1500 years later, we can transcreate it for modern men and women. Krishna, as an Avatara is mythologically one of the 10 incarnations of the God Vishnu on Earth, as was the Buddha.

I have kept the commentary minimal so as not to interrupt the flow of the poetry. Occasionally, there are knotty points, when paradox is used as a teaching method. The Gita can be taken on many levels. I have not taken it as a conventional religious text. I do, however, grant that spiritual practice is emphasized as a first necessary stage to focus attention and concentration before "letting go." I have rather tried to emphasize where it points out the more advanced spiritual teaching leading to Advaita Vedanta or non-dualism. In the last chapter there is a complete surrender leading to Self-Realization. The Gita gives us an insight into the principles alive in the magnificent Vedic culture of the Saraswati Valley. This culture was truly aristocratic in the real sense and its knowledge affected the other civilizations of the Ancient World. Also one has to distinguish, as did Shankara, between the para vidya (esoteric doctrine) and the apara vidya (exoteric, lower doctrine). The Gita mixes them up in many chapters.

In this transcreation, a modern term for the invigoration of the original text, the emphasis is on giving the reader a flavor of the poetic literary dimension while retaining the essential meaning. This is a technique the late Poet Laureate, Ted Hughes, employed with Ovid, Seamus Heaney with *Beowulf* and Coleman Barkes with the works of Jalladin Rumi. Various verses have been greatly expanded into poems with heaps of metaphors to bring home the point.

The Gita is meant to be thoroughly enjoyed. Its continuous reading implants a seed in the psyche to bring about a transformation of the life. One should not puzzle too much over philosophy. The reading will do its work without interference by the monkey mind. As the great sage Ramana Maharshi told a questioner who asked, "Should we read the Gita every day?" He replied, "Yes, always."[2]

The commentary is an amalgamation of my own understanding based on studying the major commentaries of Shankara, Aurobindo, Jnaneshwar, Ramesh Balsekar, Arthur Osborne, Professor Radhakrishnan and Swami Chidbharanada, amongst others, but in my own words and from my own experience.

Briefly, the Gita leads to Self-Realization when through Grace, the ego's identification with the mind-body is ended. A shift in perspective takes place to the Witnessing Consciousness. There are three stages, firstly that of intellectual understanding, then spiritual practice, and finally surrender.

*   *   *

All of the current Western Advaita teachers[3] underwent this preliminary step of spiritual practice, and made great efforts initially.

---

[2] Ramana Maharshi's Gospel, Chapter IV, *Spiritual Teachings of Ramana Maharshi*, Shambala, 1971.
[3] For further details see *Teachers of the One* by Paula Marvelly, Watkins Publishing.

Papaji was a Krishna Bhakta of many years' standing before he met Ramana Maharshi.

Ramesh Balsekar spent 20 years with a traditional guru before he met Nisargadatta Maharaj.

Catherine Ingram practiced Vipassana Meditation for 17 years before she met Papaji.

Tony Parsons spent 20 years with Osho "therapies" after his event in the park.

Francis Lucille worked with Jean Klein for 20 years, from about the time of his understanding.

Mira Pagal de Coux spent six years with Papaji as his wife and companion.

Wayne Liquorman practiced Buddhist meditation and yoga before meeting Ramesh.

Robert Adams was three years with Ramana Maharshi after he woke up during a math class, and he spent many years after that visiting and observing other sages and their disciples, quietly.

Pamela Wilson studied the Sedona Method with Lester Levonson for many years, and was a devotee of Robert Adams afterwards.

The list is endless but in every case the Source arranges suitable preparation for us. The main exception is Ramana Maharshi who did no spiritual practice before Grace gave him Self-Realization at the age of 16.

It has been suggested to me by Pamela Wilson that the stress on spiritual practice at the beginning, in the Gita, benefited the whole "collective consciousness" of the Satsanga. The books of Dr David Frawley emphasize and give guidance on spiritual practice which supports Self-Realization.

*   *   *

Perhaps I should relate my qualifications for engaging in a book such as this.

The year was 1953, and aged 23 I married my teenage sweetheart. I was rapturously happy, had a good job, and was setting up a simple home. I wished to thank God for my happiness, and prayed earnestly, devotedly, to be able to live a truly religious life, even in the grossly materialistic twentieth century.

My good father had a strong religious faith. We were neo-orthodox Jews, and I took my Judaism very seriously. I had also received strong Christian influences in my education. I had come to the conclusion that there must be something more to conventional religion than Anglo-Judaism in the 1950s. I started to search comparative religions: Islam, Christianity, Buddhism, and Hinduism. I felt strongly drawn to the Sanatana Dharma, and read avidly the background to this great religion. I found myself for some reason on my own starting Hatha Yoga practice, meditation, and coloring a Sri Chakra Yantra (a mandala), which attracted me enormously. I was intellectually impressed by Aldous Huxley's conversion to Hinduism through the Ramakrishna Vedanta movement. Huxley was a boyhood hero of mine.

Then one morning, after finishing a yoga practice and shoulder stand, I suddenly experienced a transcendental feeling of great strength. The silent sound, almost barely vocalized, of "Who Am I?" enveloped me inwardly and outwardly for several minutes. It was tremendous and awe-inspiring.

I was transfixed, almost bowled over. I wondered what had happened. I knew beyond doubt that this was a major religious experience. It seemed the answer to my prayer "to lead a truly religious life" – the search for "Whom Am I." I had never heard of Ramana at this time, and did not relate the experience to any specific teaching, but to Almighty God and His command to discover my true identity.

Then a series of miraculous events happened. I was strongly led to meet Kenneth Walker, a leading member of the Gurdjieff Movement in the UK. I read P. D. Ouspensky's and Maurice Nicholl's books, and was captivated.

Here I felt was an answer about how to live a truly religious life – *The Fourth Way*, based on effort, psychological understanding, Self-observation, Self-remembering and study. I then discovered *Talks of Ramana Maharshi* in Watkins Bookshop. I now knew where my "Who Am I" experience had come from, and who was the Master behind my experience, my secret guide, answering my prayer. I read most of the Ramana literature. I stayed with Gurdjieff until 1971.

In 1971, although I was very grateful for all I had learned in the way of spiritual methods, under J. Krishnamurti's influence I realized his critique of hierarchical authoritarian religious organizations was broadly correct, and led to hypocrisy. I followed K earnestly, and attended his talks in England and Switzerland whenever possible. I read his books, practiced his choiceless awareness and Self-observational approach. I had found a living master and was deeply impressed by his life and spiritual stature. My wife agreed with my new direction, and also attended the talks. I started a study group in London with another K devotee, based on K's teachings.

I was still living in my head. My heart was closed for some reason. I became ill for the first time in my life, and on my sick bed my wife gave me a magazine *Yoga and Health* (under K's influence I now attended regular Hatha Yoga classes). In it was a photo of Ramana and an article on his teaching.

I looked at the picture. It was full of love and compassion, it spoke the answer to my prayer, "Come to me, come to me, you are ready." I now fully recognized that he always had been my true master. I vowed to devote my whole life to Bhagavan and his teaching, to study it and practice it earnestly, and surrender to him as best as I could. Around that time my wife died suddenly from an unexpected cerebral hemorrhage. I was devastated but surrendered in faith to Bhagavan and the Will of God. I knew she had not really died, as the Gita says.

I was introduced to Jean Klein and Douglas Harding shortly thereafter. From these two important teachers I learned the real meaning of Advaita experientially. After a workshop with Douglas at Nacton, I again had the same experience of "Who Am I?" that had welled up very strongly in 1953. My Master Bhagavan confirmed his presence and the practice. I was surprised at how long my preparation with Gurdjieff and Krishnamurti had to be before I recognized my *full entire* devotion to Him. Later that year I was receiving some Alexander Technique lessons, and had the same "Who Am I?" experience again. All doubts had been dispelled.

After meeting Lucia Osborne at a Jean Klein meeting, I started a small Ramana Maharshi Study Group with a few friends in London, and eventually visited India and the Ashram in 1984. Bhagavan had silently led me since my first prayer to God, and now directed me to Arunachala and confirmed my practice. I have never swerved from my vow since, and he has taught me "Diving into the Heart" so my sadhana progresses through his infinite Grace. After visits to Ramanasraman and becoming Chair of the Ramana Foundation UK, I have made an extensive study of Ramana Maharshi's teachings as well as the scriptural basis of Advaita Vedanta, which includes the Bhagavad Gita.

It is my sincere wish that all who read this auspicious scriptural poem will benefit spiritually.

Alan Jacobs
London 2003

I

The grief of Arjuna

1   The blind king Dhritarashtra inquired:

Now King Pandu's wrathful sons
Are raged 'gainst mine in war
On the sacred field of righteousness,
Tell me what took place, Sanjaya?

The blind king Dhritarashtra is keen to learn what is happening now that there is to be a battle between his son's army and the outraged Pandavas led by Arjuna. The sons of the blind king had been grossly insulted by the Pandavan Prince. Their sister, Draupadi, had been humiliated and almost dishonored by them. Enmity built up between the two royal families who were in conflict, inevitably leading to war. Krishna had attempted to make peace but to no avail.

He decided to assist the Pandavas and graciously volunteered to be Arjuna's charioteer. He felt the Pandavas were in the right.

The battle took place on the Field of Kurukshetra. This was also allegorically the Field of Dharma. It implies an esoteric significance that the battle can be seen as an inner warfare between Dharma (righteous harmony) and Adharma (unrighteous disharmony). Krishna and Arjuna are within us. The Gita points the way to righteous harmony. The King of Adharma (the Kurus) is symbolically blind.

The divine Krishna is a king, mentioned historically in the Upanishads. In this poem he is both an historic figure and an embodiment of Divine Wisdom, an Avatar. Thus the Gita is the literary image of Lord Krishna, both as an historic figure and often as a personification of the Divine.

Most scholars date the Gita compilation to be approximately 500 BCE. It is in fact an Upanashadic anthology in 18 chapters[1], a sacred number in Hinduism. It is possible Lord Krishna was the compiler, a tradition and duty of kings.

Sanjaya describes the Battle Royal. Sanjaya spoke. The sage, Vyasa, miraculously gave the courtier a special clairvoyant power in order for him to be able to relate what was happening in the battle to his blind king.

2–4   Seeing the vast Pandava army
       Your son, Prince Duryodhana,
       Approached his revered teacher Drona,
       A cunning bowman of arch-skill,
       And said: "Look at the huge army
       Rallied by the Pandava Princes,
       There are many brave soldiers

---

[1] Appendix 3 gives the significance of the mystic number 18.

And archers, equal to our Bhisma
Led by their noble chief Arjuna.
I am concerned, and
Seek your advice."

These opening verses dramatically paint the scene of tension and crisis brought about by what is to become a bloody civil war between rival royal families. The leading Chiefs are named. Under the Laws of Manu, the great code which governed Ancient India, the warriors were the aristocrats second only to the Brahman priests. It was their sacred duty to defend the Dharma, the state of righteous harmony in the kingdom.

5   There sits gallant Yudhamanu
The two kings, Visvata and Kashi,
The sons of Beautiful Draupadi,
All wielding sword, spear, and mace.
With their soldiers they lead
A galaxy of golden chariots
Hosting man-eating tigers, keen to kill.

6–11   There is the mighty Bhisma,
Our Chief. His breastplate
Blazing like the radiant Sun.

12–13   Then Bhisma blew on his conch shell,
A rallying call to all his troops,
The footmen sounded cow horns,
And drummed tattoos on their shields.
Trumpets and tabors added to the din,

The battle horses reared,
Neighing, snorting, champing,
The hullabaloo of war
Roared like the jungle
Throughout the land.

14–15 Then Lord Krishna and Prince Arjuna
Raised themselves up in their gilded Chariot.
Krishna cracked his driver's whip
And held his twin white chargers back.
They both raised conch shells to their lips,
And blew the sacred sound of Aum.

Krishna's conch is symbolically the matrix of the five elements (earth, air, fire, water, and ether). This is central to the
Gita's theory of how matter is manifested, a juxtaposition
of elements, the substratum of which is Consciousness. The
Aum is the primeval sound from which Creation emerges.
The horses drawing Krishna's chariot are the wild senses, he
is the intelligence controlling them with the whip of rigor
when needed. Both armies, by making a tumultuous battle-
roar, steadied their nerves and terrified their opponents at
the same time.

16–18 Prince Yudhisthirya joined in with his conch,
As did his warriors, bowmen, and knights.

These verses are mainly lists of names. Most translators
group them together, omit some, and simplify them as I
have done.

19 The deafening roar of war
Sank deep into Earth's molten core,
And was even overheard by
The Gods in the heavens,
The roar sent a harsh message
Ripping through the hearts of
The enemy.

20 Arjuna hoisted his flag
Which showed Hanuman,
The powerful Monkey God,
Who assisted Rama
To beat the demon King
Ravanna,
And save his Queen Sita
In the emerald Isle of Lanka.
He gazed at the sons of
Dhritarashtra
In awesome battle formation.
The flight of missiles was about
To start.
The mighty archer Arjuna
Lifted his giant bow
As an act of defiance.

21–23 Then addressing Lord
Krishna
He asked him to guide their Chariot
To rest between the foes,
So he might see these many men

Lusting for battle,
Whom, by duty, he was ordained
To fight.

24–25   So Krishna steered the chariot
And halted between the armies,
In front of Bhisma, Drona, and
Their allies.
Arjuna saw all the Kurus
Raised like a mighty iron fist
Poised to strike.

26   Arjuna gazing at his enemies
With full attention
Saw many blood relations
Among them.

27   Seeing his family at war
He was flooded by sorrow,
As if some tidal wave had struck.
He was like a mother grieving
Over a child who had just died.
Despairingly he spoke to Krishna.

28–30   Krishna, I see my own kinsmen
Keen to kill each other in war.
My knees shake, my mouth
Is dry
As a sand blasted desert.
My hair stands on end,

My skin is on fire.
Even my great bow Gandara
Has dropped from my grasp.
I'm giddy and dazed,
My thoughts whirl in anguish,
My stomach is tight with fear.

31–32 I see evil signs in all this.
I can't see anything good
From killing my own kinsfolk.
I do not want victory,
Nor the pleasure of winning
Like some schoolboy bully.
Of what use is beating them?

33 Those for whom I once
Desired happiness
Are now staking their wealth
And lives.

34 These are my dear teachers,
My blood relations,
Oh why, oh why, oh why?

35 I do not want to kill them
Like blind rats in a trap,
Point blank, I tell you now,
This is how I feel, Krishna.

36 After slaughtering them

Only guilt, shame,
And remorse
Will be left for me.

37   It's bad to kill our cousins.
How can this ever make us happy?

38–39   Even if their thoughts, blackened
By greed and lust,
Like hungry dogs on heat,
See nothing wrong in destruction
Of the family circle,
And nothing wrong in dark treachery,
Should not we, Krishna, be wise
And turn away from evil?

40   On the ending of a family,
Its old righteous harmony
Dies and then unrighteous
Disharmony will rule
With fatal results.

41   When this prevails, the
Women become corrupt,
Ending up as money grabbing whores.
This disease infects the breed
And aristocrats marry servant girls.

42   They will descend to hell.
Our heritage will fall

In ruin.
No one will praise them
With offerings ever again.

43 So these evil deeds,
Destroying family bonds,
Undermine society
And its stability.
It is like removing the
Corner stones
Of an ancient temple.
It will collapse!

44 We know that hell
Is the home of these folk
When family harmony
Is broken up.

45 What a sin on which we are
Hell bent,
To kill our cousins
Through desire for the
Joy of triumph.

46 Better for me were
The Kuru sons,
Swords in hand to slay me
Unarmed and unresisting.

47 Arjuna rested.

Sanjaya concluded.
So having finished his speech
Arjuna threw down his bow,
Sank in his chariot seat
Bent in despair.
He wept with grief.

II

The philosophy and
its practice

*The Sankya, India's most ancient philosophic system revealed by
the sage Kapila is similar to the Yoga of Patanjali.*

In Chapter II, Krishna, in his role of Avatar, unveils the
divine wisdom leading to Self-Realization and the teaching
of the essential spiritual need for the first step of practice
in order to gain necessary powers of attention and focus,
accompanied by intellectual understanding, leading to surrender and enlightenment through Grace.

1–2   Sanjaya continues speaking to his king;
       Arjuna, overcome by awful grief,
       Starts to weep, his heavy heart melts
       With pity, as salt melts in the sea,

Or as clouds are swept by winds.
He stammers like a black swan trapped in deep
    mud.
Seeing the Prince overwhelmed, Lord Krishna
    spoke compassionately.

In this verse, the metaphors have been adapted from
Jnanenshwar's greatly expanded poetic commentary on the
Gita. This is a masterly work by the child prodigy, thirteenth-
century Marathi Saint and Jnani. It sets the narrative so that
Krishna's admonition and discourse to Arjuna can proceed.
Ramana Maharshi was once asked by a questioner to
nominate the most important verses of the Gita, as 700 were
too difficult to absorb. The Maharshi obliged by reciting 40.[1]
He began with this verse omitting Chapter I, which largely
relates to the historic battle setting.

2   From where does this revolting weakness
    Unworthy of a soldier spring?
    It's as if a huge, black boulder blocked
    Your noble path to valor and Vedic virtue.

This verse begins Lord Krishna's stern rebuke to shake him
out of its conventional depression, which paralyzes action,
"Hamlet's disease." The metaphors come from various commentaries which all emphasize Krishna's apparent harshness
as the only cure for the illness of "why should this happen
to me?"

3   No Prince! Lance this poisonous
    Abscess of cringing, degrading fear.

[4] These verses, forty-two in this version, are set out in a table in Appendix 1.

Throw off the foul cloak of cowardice,
Wake up! Just be your own true Self,
Gird up your loins
Be the whip lash of your foes.

Krishna continues to upbraid Arjuna in no uncertain terms.
He must "pull himself together" and with determination
play his part in the war and be the scourge of his enemies.
Sri Ramakrishna the Parahamsa used to say, "He who is
soft and weak-minded like the puffed rice soaked in milk,
is good for nothing. He cannot achieve anything great. But
the strong and virile one is heroic. He is the accomplisher of
everything in life." This verse is apposite to the "Way of the
Householder," the Gita's teaching as is the "Way of Advaita"
taught by Sri Ramana Maharshi. It is often described as the
"Way of the Hero." The true hero breaks the conventional
modes of morality to realize the truth.

To this harsh rebuke Arjuna replied:

4   But how in the fierce fire of battle
Dare I shoot barbed arrows at beloved Drona,
My dear teacher and preceptor.
And Bhisma, my own blood relation?
These are my highly respected elders,
Both are noble, honorable men
Worthy of my reverence too.

How have the dank, polluted waters
Of hyper-melancholic self-pity,
And chronically dark depression,

Abysmal sentimental grief,
Sunk me into this foul swamp, my dear Krishna?

Arjuna is faced with a severe moral crisis, which often faces
people in the world of apparent reality. He continues to
stress the enormity of the problem which agonizes him. He
goes on:

4   So, Krishna,
     I repeat,
     How can I kill
     Bhisma and Drona?
     It beggars belief!

5   Yes it must be better to live on stale crusts,
     Like some wretched gutter beggar,
     With all my loved ones still alive,
     Than eat a meal of their caked blood,
     Suffering rat-gnawing guilt
     For what remains of one's life?

Arjuna uses powerful metaphors to emphasize the anguish
he feels in the hope that Lord Krishna will point the way to
a solution. He continues.

6   What is worse here?
     Who in heaven or earth really knows?
     To be the triumphant winner, and cheer hooray!
     Or be the miserable, poor loser, doom and gloom.
     Many will attack me fiercely with their spite,
     As these deaths will surely end our family
          happiness.

Each verse adds to the dramatic tension weighing on Arjuna's heavily burdened mind. He pleads for relief from Lord Krishna whom he knows to be a fully enlightened being.

7   Totally perplexed and confused
      I wrestle like a trapped bear
      In some inhuman pit or snare.
      My scattered thoughts turn to you for help.
      I don't know what can heal my dread,
      Now engraved into my heart and head.

Arjuna has not completed his peroration. He adds to his argument with exaggerated similes and ends in despair.

8   Even if I were the emperor of the whole world,
      An all-conquering demi-god,
      And my many enemies scattered,
      I do not see what could ever end my sorrow.

9   Sanjaya comments to his blind king:
      So Arjuna appealed to Lord Krishna,
      Crying out "I shall *never, ever* fight!"
      And waiting, held his silence.

Arjuna ends his appeal and awaits the response from the all-wise Lord Krishna. The tension is enormous as Krishna is slowly driving the chariot between the serried ranks of the opposing armies in full battle array. Krishna responds in immortal words.

10   Lord Krishna smiled with compassion,

Steering carefully between the two opposing
armies.
While Arjuna wept in bitter despair,
Krishna then spoke most profoundly.

11 Fool! You are grieving where no grief should ever
be!
You speak words totally empty of any wisdom,
For the truly, truly, wise at heart,
Never grieve for those that are alive,
And never ever grieve for those that die.

This is one of the key sentences in the entire Gita. Krishna
points out that *grief* is folly and *wisdom* is *not to grieve*. The
rationale of this is to be expanded. Krishna is essentially
informing Arjuna that worrying is totally unnecessary and
never a wise action, it only saps our substantial energy leading to impotence and failure to act intelligently.

12 There never has been such a time.
When I or you did not exist
Neither these lords and kings nor me.
Nor shall there ever be a time
When we shall ever cease to be!

Krishna held that each individual Consciousness is imperishable as Consciousness is co-existent with the whole universe.
As the Christian saint, Suso, put it: "All creatures have ex-
isted eternally in the Divine essence as in their exemplar. So
far as they conform to the Divine idea, all beings were before

their creation, one with the essence of God." In a sense God as Consciousness-Awareness-Self is the totality of all empirical existence imbued with the One Consciousness.

13   To man's fine intellect and brain,
      Set in a vain monkey's body,
      First comes puking, muling childhood,
      Then lusty, adventurous youth,
      Then ever perishing old age,
      In this House of Life, and others.
      The sages know this to be the truth,
      And they never, ever fear their Death.

The best comment on this verse is the short metrical assonant rhymed poem Sir Edwin Arnold inserted in his otherwise blank verse Gita:

      Nay, but as when he layeth
      His worn-out robes away,
      And, taking new ones, sayeth,
      "These will I wear today!
      So putteth by the spirit
      Lightly its garb of flesh,
      And passeth to inherit
      A residence afresh."

Modern science says that every seven years all the cells in the body are renewed. We are in a state of constant flux. We change every moment, but behind the change of age stands the immortal undying Self, Pure Consciousness. Look at an early photograph of yourself and you will be convinced of this Truth. He who looks at the photo is the same Consciousness although the face has now aged. The work of Douglas Harding, the English sage emphasizes this point by mirror experiments.[2]

14   All that agitates your mind and senses,
      Brings up blushes or flushes,
      Deep sorrows or fleeting joys,
      They are brief my friend, and ever changing.

Ramesh Balsekar the contemporary Mumbai sage has selected the 70 most significant verses of the Gita with a masterful commentary. There is a table in Appendix 2. This is his first choice. He writes: "If the changing responses of the senses are seen in this perspective they lose their influence to cause undue pleasure and pain. One can accept the changes with equanimity." This introduces the law of opposites. The psyche is based on opposite responses; the pendulum of feelings swings between like and dislike, delight and suffering, ad infinitum. This must be clearly witnessed and understood to be free of the tyranny of these emotional and intellectual swings between polarities.

15   So bear with it, as the wise bear it!
      The soul which is unmoved and strong
      With constant calm, like a rock in a storm
      Accepts all sorrows and joys equally.

As Thomas à Kempis puts it so well in his *Imitation of Christ*.

---

[2] Douglas Harding has written many books available through Penguin-Arkana and more recently with Watkins Publishing.

The desires of the senses draw us hither and thither,
But when the hour is past,
What do they bring us but remorse of conscience and
dissipation of spirit?

It is clear that Krishna's advice to Arjuna is to be aware of
the opposites and to transcend them.

16   So dwell in your Eternal Self,
     Pure Consciousness, Awareness, Peace,
     "What is" will never cease to be.
     To see the truth between the existent
     And the non-existent
     Is given to those who discriminate.
     Substance can never be its shadow.

Krishna's masterly advice is to keep *quiet and rest in the
Self whose nature is Divine*. The Self is defined as pure
Chit-Sat-Ananda or Consciousness, Awareness, Peace. That
which does not materialize can never exist, and that which
does, never ceases to be. Discrimination is the capacity to see
the difference between the essence of a thing in itself and its
mere happening, as an object in process, like in Plato's cave
where the shadows are not the reality.

The essence or "thing in itself" is Real. Happenings are just
moving shadows on the screen of Consciousness, Awareness,
the Self.

17   Comprehend that I, the Consciousness,
     Which envelopes and impregnates all matter,
     Can never be destroyed by any means,
     It is unchangeable for ever and ever.

18 Know clearly Arjuna
    This body is mortal,
    Dies and rots in the grave
    Or is burned on a pyre,
    Or incinerated in a crematorium.
    But that Consciousness
    Which lives in your body
    Never dies and is infinite
    So Arjuna, I urge you
    With all my might
    To fight! Fight! Arjuna!
    Fight! Fight!

19–21 One man believes he is the killer,
       The other believes he has been killed.
       This is the height of ignorance,
       I tell you Arjuna,
       There has never been a killer
       Or anyone killed.
       You, Arjuna, were ever, ever
       Born as Consciousness, the Self,
       You have never changed as
       That Consciousness,
       You are unborn, eternal,
       Infinite, that is your Divine Nature.
       You never die when your body dies.
       Only the body dies,
       Brain, bones, and blood.
       Realizing, recognizing,
       Knowing That which

Consciousness Is, as
Indestructible, Eternal,
Infinite, unborn, unchanging,
How can you ever kill
Or another ever kill the unkillable?

Once one sees that what we are is Consciousness and not the body, it all makes sense.

22 Just as you toss away
Worn out clothes and buy new ones,
So when the body is worn out
A new one is found for
The Self who lives within Consciousness.

The Gita now introduces the doctrine of rebirth. At the lowest level this is called reincarnation – at the most advanced level of understanding it does not exist. Let us use the authority of Ramana Maharshi, the universally acknowledged sage, whose exemplary life led to the renaissance of Advaita Vedanta in the twentieth century. The reincarnation theory stressed in the Gita gives psychological comfort. Ramana, as a concession to his questions, used to say it is as true as you believe it to be. In fact this theory is a very intelligent psychological device inserted by the authors of the Gita. The doctrine that social good deeds will lead you to heaven, but bad deeds will send you to hell, has preserved Indian society for thousands of years without the need of police; police were a British invention in the nineteenth century. We must look deeper into this mystery – and it is a mystery – nobody has returned from the dead to tell us what happens. Transmigration is an intermediate position, which will be discussed as the commentary proceeds.

Let me now quote Ramana Maharshi.

Q. Do you mean to say that I was never even born?

A. Yes, you are now thinking that you are the body and therefore confuse yourself with its birth and death. But you are not the body and you have no birth and death (as Consciousness).

Q. So you do not uphold the theory of rebirth?

A. No. I want to remove your confusion that you will be reborn. It is you who thinks that you will be reborn.

As he taught that theories about reincarnation are based on the false assumption that the individual entity is real. Once this illusion is understood, that the individual is a mind-body system in Consciousness, then after-death theories collapse. Out of compassion and as a concession to ignorant questioners, and rather than destroy their faith by feeding them with more than they could understand, he would say that if one *imagined* the individual self to be real then eventually it might identify with a new body. But once identification with the mind-body ends then reincarnation theories do not apply. In these opening chapters the Gita talks about rebirth and it is a doctrine that has great ethical and moral benefits. The sages knew how to govern the majority.

However, of course, new mind-body organizations are being continuously created for the great "play" of life and death. As Ramesh Balsekar, a devotee of Ramana Maharshi, writes in his commentary on the Gita II.22: "The impersonal consciousness casts off worn-out body mind equipments and enters into new ones as part of general evolution." This implies that at death the subtle body of residual life memories returns to the "pool of Consciousness" and Consciousness has now many qualities to transmigrate into new lives for its own continuance of the "dream of life," or Lila. Inborn talents and tendencies may appear in a new life and residual memories of a past one imagined. This explains child prodigies. Transmigration of souls or subtle bodies is a more tenable theory than reincarnation of egos. Egotism is a product of the brain and rots at death. Consciousness and the subtle body (feelings) leave the body at death and re-enter the pool of Consciousness for the possibility of new actors on the stage of life as we experience it.

23–24   Consciousness, the Self,
       Cannot be pierced
       By swords or arrows,
       Water cannot wet it,
       Fire cannot burn it,
       Nor can the winds dry it.

Consciousness or the Self can be understood as a screen on which the play of life appears. As in a motion picture or television show, the screen is unaffected by what takes place on it. Bombs explode, floods, wars, and violent death happen in the cinema and on TV, but the screen is unaffected.

25   Consciousness is
      Everlasting,
      All pervading,
      Changeless,
      Motionless.

26   It is beyond thought,
      Knowing all this
      Never, ever, ever grieve!

27   Even if you think
      There are more and more
      Being born
      And then dying
      Still you should not grieve.

28   For he, who is born,
      Death is certain.
      To him, who dies,
      Death is certain.
      Never grieve for
      What is absolutely certain.

By grief is meant all forms of depression and anxiety. It must
be understood that every event that happens is ordained by
the inscrutable Source and must be wholeheartedly accepted
rather than "grieved over."

29   Death must happen
      For all creatures alive
      From atom to stella-nova,
      Slug beetle to holy saint,
      So rebirth is a new form
      Of Consciousness.
      Death happens to all.
      Sentient beings –
      They are not there at first,
      And then they are,
      And then not again.
      What is there to grieve
      In all this, I ask you?

30 The full glory of the True Self,
    Consciousness, Awareness, Peace,
    Is only known by a few.
    Few try to describe
    The indescribable.
    A few listen to my teaching
    But very few reach its understanding.

31 Consciousness, in all living
    Beings,
    Dwells in their body.
    It is eternal
    And can never be harmed.
    So never, ever, grieve!
    Remember the way
    Of righteous, harmonious duty.
    Never flinch from it.
    There is no greater good
    For a warrior
    Than to fight for a just cause.
    That is his duty!

32 Happy are the warriors
    For whom a just war
    Comes unsought.
    It is an open door to heaven.

33 A warrior's happiness
    Lies not in the home pleasures
    Of wife and children,

But in fighting for a
Rightful cause.

The way of the warrior here is to destroy evil. If Britain
and America had not fought Fascism, the world would have
fallen to an even lower level, just as the Western world is
currently waging a war against international terrorism.

34–35   If you shirk the fight
         Your fellow warriors
         Will despise you
         For cowardice.
         Dishonor to a warrior
         Is worse than death!

36   Your enemies will abuse you
      With scorpion tongues.
      Your manhood will be questioned.
      This is a grievous matter.
      Like the son who fails
      To defend his father.

37   But if you fight,
      Then slain,
      You will reach heaven,
      Or victorious,
      You shall be honored
      On Earth.
      Rise therefore Arjuna,
      Gird up your loins,

Like a lion defending
His pride
And fight!

38 Whether or not the future
Holds pleasure or pain,
Winning or losing,
With brave equanimity,
Prepare to fight,
Be sinless in the eyes of men.

39 This I have told you
Is the wisdom of philosophy.
Now I shall tell you
The wisdom of Yoga
Which shall free you
From the bonds of action.

Philosophy is the "Samkhya" transcended by the reality of
the Self. Yoga is broadly based on the Sutras of Patanjali.

40 In this path
Efforts are never in vain.
No obstacle prevails,
Even a little of the righteous harmonious way
Saves one from fear.

Ramana Maharshi said there is no Grace without effort and
no effort without Grace. Effort means "from the brave" ie
from our strong part overcoming weak tendencies.

41   The bold are single-minded.
     The minds of the fearful
     Are divided and scattered.
     Like ant hills
     After they are stepped on.

42   The ignorant are attached
     To the mere letter and law
     Of the Scriptures.
     They declare
     In flowery language
     That there is nothing beyond.

43   In bondage to their desires
     They crave a carnal paradise.
     They seek rebirth for
     The fruit of their actions
     And perform rituals
     To gain pleasure and power.

44   Constantly driven
     By craving for
     Sensual gratification
     And power
     Their minds are enslaved
     By words.
     They fail to rest in meditation.

45–48   The Vedas speak
        Of three tendencies

But be free of them.
Be free, too, of polarities
Which entrap the mind
Swinging between
Opposites.
Pleasure, pain,
Cruelty, kindness,
Love, hate,
Charity, indifference,
And so on to infinity.
Be free of wanting
To gain goods.
Be stable in the
Supreme spirit
Possessed only by Consciousness
The Self.
The seed is in thy breed
Oh warrior, hero, Prince.

This is a most important verse. The insights into the human psyche of the Ancient Rishis are shown to Arjuna. We are governed by three alternating states or Gunas. These states are Rajas, Tamas, and Sattva. The Rajistic state is passionately active, the Tamastic is lethargically passive, the Sattvic is one of clarity and equanimity. The Gita talks about these states, which alternate like the weather, and are largely beyond our control. They are compounded by the polarity swings between the opposites, the contrary emotional attitudes that co-exist together. We may be kind today and cruel tomorrow, happy one hour and sad the next, clear-sighted one minute and confused the next. Ad infinitum. The play of the Gunas is fully discussed in chapters XVI, XVII and XVIII, of the Gita. Krishna advises transcending the play of the Gunas and the polarities, so as to rest in the Sattvic state, close to the Self of Consciousness. A process of self-observation, witnessing or noticing this structure impartially is a preliminary stage, before concentration and attention become more developed and focused, with practice, either in a group or alone.

49   Despicable, disgusting,
       To be totally abhorred,
       Are those "hypocrites" whose
       Desires yearn for a sensual paradise
       As a reward for their actions.
       One who has reached
       This profound understanding
       Transcends the naive
       Concepts of what is "good" and what is "evil."

These verses are the teaching of the Yoga of Knowledge. They stems from the sage, Kapila, later to be synthesized by Patanjali in his famous Sutras.

This yoga is not the conventional Hatha Yoga, which is the work of the body to attain a so-called Sattvic state, but is abused by those who are seeking slim figures, longer life, or fugitive health. It is closer to Raja Yoga as taught by Vivekananda, the disciple of Ramakrishna, Parahamsa.

The Sankhya (philosophy) and the Patanjali (yoga) combine in Krishna's teachings both to be enlarged and transcended. The Gita may be viewed as an arrow aimed at our heart – as with Arjuna – confused and perplexed. When we turn round "Metanoia" we see Krishna as our Self, and we may read the Gita as if we are Him. He is the intelligent still voice of the interest in the Self behind us all as wisdom. The Consciousness, Awareness, is only impeded by the "I am the mind-body" idea; some imaginary entity called Alan, or Tom, Dick, Harry, Jane, Mary, and so on, ad infinitum.

Victory is now, or else in this life we suffer to be recycled into the pool of consciousness to form another body – to suffer again and hopefully realize the Truth eventually – so, why not now?

When the Maharshi was questioned as to how he realized the Truth at 16 without a Sadhana (spiritual practice or a guru) he said it must have been because of a previous life. He never said *his* life but a previous life. This leaves it to Source to ordain beings for its own Lila (or dramatic play) whether they be Ramana Maharshi or even a psychopathic personality. This is the radical Truth which Ramesh Balsekar,[3] a devotee of Ramana in giving his advanced teaching, constantly emphasizes.

The subtle body transmigrated is not the same ego of the last life. It may have admixtures from other lives. A new "I" is formed which may, in rare cases, remember past lives or display prodigious talents. Yet all is according to Divine Will – mysterious and inscrutable as it is – so be it beyond human understanding. What we can infer safely is that there is a transmigration of a subtle body not a reincarnation of the same egotistic "I conceit" which dies with the death of the brain and its decomposition.

50   One who has been given
      This understanding

---

[3] Ramesh Balsekar has written many books in his own hand. *The Final Truth* or the *Ultimate Understanding*, published by Watkins Publishing, is the summation of his wisdom.

Transcends the childish
Ideas of good and bad.

Good and evil are relative concepts; relative to the human condition. As Shakespeare said: "There is nothing good or bad but thinking makes it so." In fact, all emerges from God, Self, Consciousness, Awareness, Peace. No one can understand the ways of the creative intelligence, which govern the whole universe perfectly – as long as we believe we are separate from the whole. The human being is connected to the Divine Source. He can sing, laugh, paint, talk, reason, love, write poetry or music – which no animal can approach except as a distorted beam of this sunlight. This is in spite of his fiendish rush into pleasure and relief from his intrinsic pain center born from the frustration of the ego.

51   If the fruits of action
       Are renounced
       One is free from
       The idea of rebirth
       And free from sorrow.

52   When your impish
       Monkey mind
       Has crossed
       The deep pit of delusion
       You will no longer
       Care one way or another
       About the fruits of action.

53   When your poor mind,

Which is only a
Faggot of thoughts,
Is confused by scripture,
Stand firm instead,
Steadfast,
Focusing attention
On the Self as Consciousness,
You will then see the Truth
Of my teaching.

54 Arjuna asked Lord Krishna:
Tell me what a man is like
Who is firm in wisdom
And has powers of attention
And concentration?
How does one who is steadfast talk,
How does he sit,
How does he walk?

55 Krishna answered.
When a man throws out desires
Like so much dirty linen,
Stained, smelly, and grubby,
And is happy in himself
He is a sage, steadfast in wisdom.

56 He who never despairs in grief,
Controlled, in pleasure,
For whom, fear and anger
Have swiftly fled like a deer herd which has

Sensed a tiger
He is a sage of steadfast wisdom.

57   Unattached,
Accepting so called good and bad
Equally,
Without exultation or disgust,
He is a sage of steadfast
Wisdom.

58   He who can withdraw
His senses
By focused attention
From the glamour of objects,
As the tortoise withdraws
His limbs
Into his shell.
He is a sage of steadfast wisdom.

59   Sense objects flee,
From whoever stops
Wallowing like a pig
In a carnal trough.
If this hidden glitter
Lingers,
Then having a glimpse
Of Supreme Reality
As Consciousness, Awareness, Peace,
It will vanish
As the early morning mist flees
Before the glorious rays of the rising sun.

60 But even though the hero
    Strives wisely,
    The impetuous senses
    Often distract him by sheer force.
    Like a thundering herd
    Of wild horses in stampede.

61 Firmly directing them all
    As the charioteer controls
    His battle steeds,
    Let him stand firm,
    Pull in the reins,
    Focusing on the Self
    Which is Consciousness, Awareness, Peace.

62 Fantasies allowed to romp
    In sensuality
    Fall into a murky mire
    Leading to lusty craving.
    From this excess,
    When frustrated,
    Violent anger arises.

63 From anger springs
    Madness and delusion,
    From delusion comes
    Loss of memory,
    From loss of memory comes
    Weakness of attention,
    And from this disease
    The soul dies, dies.

64 But he too can move
Among the glittering baubles
And temptations of sensuality.
With attention controlling
The mob of his senses,
Free from wanting this
And not wanting that
He reaches the haven of peace.

65 In the calm blue mountain lake of
Stillness,
Peace,
Comes death of grief.
Attention is always there,
Living in the present moment,
The only moment there is,
The "here" and "now,"
Fully aware of Consciousness, the Self.

66 The uncontrolled
Like a horde of lemmings
Are stupid fools
Who lack the discipline
Of concentrated attention.
Without this focus there is neither peace nor
    happiness.

67 When the fool
Is dragged through the mental gutter
By the perverse, wandering mind

It whips away any
Understanding,
As storms lash a
Ship's sails
On the boundless ocean,
It capsizes.

68   So, Arjuna!
He whose senses
Are withdrawn
From the childish toys
Of glittering sense objects
Is firm in wisdom.

69   In darkest night
The sage is wide-awake
When all are awake by day
It is night for the sage.

This is one of the most cryptic and interesting verses in the whole of the Gita. It is a koanic paradox and there has been much speculation as to its actual meaning.

To people who are totally sense bound and "identified with their ego," subject to liking and disliking, then earthly things are real and they are immersed in them. They are therefore wakeful to the mundane world. But to the sage who has subdued the senses and is living from the standpoint of Consciousness and witnessing the spectacle, it is very different. His perspective is wakefulness in the night of ignorance where other beings are still subject to divine hypnosis, or the power of Maya, illusion.

70   The sage enjoys
      Perfect peace
      When all his desires
      Flow like rivers into the
      Boundless ocean,
      Leaving it calm
      But ever filled.
      This is not so with the fool
      Who continues desiring
      Even more desires.

71   He finds perfect peace
      Who sacrifices desire,
      Acting spontaneously,
      Freely,
      Appropriately,
      Serendipitously,
      Without bondage to the senses.
      Liberated from the
      Sense of "I" and "mine."
      This is the state of the sage.
      Divine.
      Free from delusion,
      Dwelling at home
      He reaches the Supreme Peace,
      Of Brahman, when Consciousness leaves the
          body.

III

Wisdom in action

*In this chapter Krishna speaks from the standpoint of the
Avatar, Jnani, or Self-Realized Being.*

Arjuna asks Lord Krishna

1   If you say
    Right understanding
    Is much better than action,
    Why on earth do
    You urge
    Me to fight in terrible wars
    When thousands may be slaughtered?

2   With such unclear logic
     You bewilder my brain,
     There must be one simple way
     To reach supreme peace?

Krishna replies:

3   Since the days of old
     A double way has been told,
     The path of knowledge
     For introverted souls,
     And for extroverts
     Like you
     The path of action.

4   Neither by giving up
     Action
     Does a man reach freedom
     From action,
     Nor by renunciation
     Of activity
     Does he reach perfection.

5   It is a hard fact,
     No one can remain
     For very long inactive!
     One is driven endlessly
     Like autumn leaves
     Blown by the wild, west wind.

6   The foolish one
     Who masters his body
     But lets his mind brood
     On sensuality,
     Like a hen hatching her chicks,
     Is nothing else but
     A hypocrite.
     A white washed can of worms.

7   He excels,
     Who masters
     His senses
     By attention
     And uses his body
     To play its predestined part
     Without attachment.

8   Perform your duty!
     Actions are better than
     No actions.
     Even saving life
     Is impossible
     Without action.

9   Worldly people are
     Chained to action,
     Slaves in irons.
     Unless the action
     Is performed as an offering
     To the Source of their own Being,

Self, Godhead, Consciousness, Awareness,
Peace.
So let your deeds be free
From attachment.
Dedicate, sanctify, sacrifice
Your acts to the Supreme
Universal Power.

10   The Source of All,
In the beginning
Created by cosmic sacrifice,
Willed that all
Should breed
And be wish fulfilling,
As the rich milk cow
Gives to her dutiful calves.

This verse has been universalized from the literal Vedic rendering.

In the beginning Prajapati (as Creator) made men together with sacrifice and said: "By this you shall propagate and it shall be your cow of plenty."

Since the Vedic civilization perished, our language has changed considerably but the essential meaning of the verse is preserved. Fifteen hundred years have passed. We must enter into the original spirit of the scriptural text.

11   Obey this principle,
And worship, love, adore
The Source of your own Being,
Inside your Heart

And outside as God, Transcendental,
Creator, Consciousness, Peace.
The two are the same
And you are one of his children
Playing the role
Ordained especially for you.
But you are not the role,
Your real Nature is the Source,
Consciousness, Awareness.
So love each other as "thy Self,"
This is a way to Supreme Peace.

Jesus said to "love thy neighbor as thy self" was the highest injunction.

12   The Good
Enjoy the food
Which remains after
The Sanctified Offering
Of thanksgiving,
But the wicked
Bolt down food
For its taste alone.
So do pigs.

Ramana Maharshi said a great aid to Self-Realization was a vegetarian diet with milk products. This leads to a Sattvic mind (clarity).

14   Beings become what they eat.
Food comes from sun, soil, and rain,

Soil and rain are sacrifices
From the Creative Source
For you.
Some call it Providence.
Sacrifice is the food for
Rightful action.

The ego is a tasty morsel to be consumed by the Self. Lord
Shiva is the high chef of "ego-cuisine." Sacrifice is the giving
up of a dearly held attachment so tyrannical egotism may be
weakened.

15   Know how action starts
From the Creative Power.
This springs from Consciousness,
So this power
Is ever present
In the sanctification
Of "what is, here and now."

16   He who in weakness
Fails to help
Push the world-wheel
In motion
Is failing in his Nature.
He is over sensual,
Steeped in pleasures
And lives in vain.

17   He who rejoices in the Self
Of Consciousness, Awareness, Peace,

Is very happy and fulfilled.
For this man and woman
There is nothing that needs
To be done.
Grace pinpoints the way.
The same power
Which made you a seeker
Will end the seeking.
In due course
Through Grace.

Ramana Maharshi said that those who come to this teaching
are already in the jaws of the tiger and certain to be consumed.
So either surrender or inquire into "who am I?" This verse
points to a transformation of conventional values. He who rejoices in the Self is free from the treadmill of compulsive action.
He can live spontaneously from the witnessing consciousness,
silent and non-judgmentally. He is the "Lily of the Field" or the
"Blue Water Lily." "He toils not, neither does he spin." This is
echoed by Taoism, amongst other traditions, as the lazy man's
way. The paradox between effort and "letting go" is perennial.

18   He does not profit
From action
Which inevitably takes place.
He has nothing to lose
Or gain.
He is independent of
Anyone for any aim
To be fulfilled
It is all the will of God.

19   So freely act the role,
      Playing all parts
      That appear to be necessary.
      By disinterested activity
      You will eventually reach
      The Self of Consciousness, Awareness, Peace.

20   It was by action
      That Great King Janaka
      Reached the Self.
      Follow his noble example!

This is an important verse. King Janaka, a historical figure in the Upanishads, was taught by the crippled sage Astavakra. The Astavakra Gita,[1] along with the Ribhu Gita, the Yoga Vashista, and the Avahuta Gita are primary non-dualistic scriptures. Ramana Maharshi used to read and study these privately with close disciples after giving concessionary answers to weary seekers. He never wished to destroy anyone's faith out of his infinite compassion – but pointed out the next step to take.

21   Whatever a sage or
      Genius does
      The mob ape,
      Hence the great marvel of King Janaka!

22   For me,
      There is no action ever

---

[1] A masterful commentary on this scripture has been written by Ramesh Balsekar called *Duet for One*, Advaita Press, CA.

Found
To be necessary
In heaven, earth, or hell,
Nor anything to reach
Or do.
Yet I act.

Heaven and hell can be seen as states of mind esoterically.

23   If I ceased
From right effortless action,
Men might
In their ignorance
Follow my lead.

24   If I ceased
From right action
Worlds would fall,
Even more social confusion
Would follow
And dire destruction
Would descend on the masses,
Even worse than is there already.

25   Just as idiots act
From attachment
So must we, the wise,
Act without attachment
As a refined example.

26   The sage must never
      Disturb
      The minds, the moral basis,
      Or the faith of the foolish,
      Who are attracted to action
      And wish for wealth
      And worship financial success
      As their only goal.
      Fortune gained by stealth,
      Followed by a sexual paradise.
      Instead he should act
      As if playing a righteous part
      On the world stage
      And urge others who come his way
      To act similarly.

27   All actions
      Are pre-determined,
      Beyond doubt,
      By the universal power
      Of natural forces,
      Confused by his false
      Sense of "I am the Doer"
      The fool stumbles and falls,
      Flat on his face.

28   But he who in wisdom
      Perceives the way natural forces work
      Is never attached.
      Knowing that it is these powers

Which act upon matter,
And get things done.

According to the Gita philosophy we must "see through" the
power of "Maya" or world illusion – the divine hypnosis and
how it operates. The world we perceive is a sensual representation monitored and interpreted by the brain. We are split-
minded, separated between knowing subject (consciousness)
and the objects seen. This is how the divine Lila, or play of life
on earth works. The philosopher, Arthur Schopenhauer, who
studied the Upanishads, makes this very clear in his book, *The
World as Will and Representation*, and explains the mechanism.
Time, space, and causality are "a priori" in the organ of cogni-
tion, the brain, and set up "Maya" or World Illusion.

29   These fools
      Misled,
      Deluded,
      Hypnotized
      By nature's magic,
      Maya,
      Become attached
      To their actions.
      But he who understands
      The All
      Should never shake
      The faith
      Of weak minds
      Or the foolish ignorant
      Who see only a very tiny part
      Of the vast cosmic scheme.

30   So fight, Arjuna!
      I implore you,
      Fight!
      Gird up thy loins,
      Man of steel,
      Hero in battle.
      Surrender all your acts
      To me
      As your teacher,
      Keep attending to thy Self,
      Consciousness, Awareness, Peace.
      Sacrifice all your worries
      Cares,
      Anxieties,
      Of the foolish "Me"
      And free yourself
      From the crazy disease
      Of doubt!
      Then take up the battle flag
      Of destiny
      And fight!

31   Those who constantly obey
      This teaching of mine,
      Submission to, and affirmation
      Of the Divine Will,
      With confidence,
      Without nit-picking intellectual
      Disputation
      But,

But,
But,
Are then freed from the
Bondage of illusory action,
The arrogant conceit to think
That "I am the Doer."
Is the Devil himself.

32　All those who hate,
Oppose,
Despise,
Object,
And reject my teaching,
Are like gluttons
Who reject healthy food
For over-spiced meats.
They are deluded as
To the true meaning of
Wisdom.
They are sentenced to
A sensual life
Of banal suffering.

33　Even the sage
Acts according to his
Disposition,
Temperament,
True nature.
All creatures
Must obey, submit

To their temperament.
What can trying to
Repress nature do
But lead to insanity?

Repression of natural instincts disastrously leads to disgrace. The number of de-frocked celibate priests beggars enumeration. The Gita is not logical in advocating chastity yet denying repression. All spiritual teaching indulges in contradiction and paradox. It is up to the aspirant to find his correct balance between two excessive opposites.

34   Each sense rejoices!
Eyes – see beauty or ugliness,
Ears – hear sublimity or noise,
Nostrils – smell perfume or stinks,
Touch – feels softness or painfulness,
Taste – savors pleasantness or poison,
Sex – find another attractive or repellent.
All have their objections,
Like and dislike,
Good and bad,
We must never be seduced
By these opposites,
The polarities,
They are huge obstacles
Impeding our path.

35   It's better to walk on one's own path
However imperfect,
Than imitate another,

Be he saint, hero, or demon,
However well acted in the part.
It's better to die
Following one's own way
Than to imitate another.
It leads to hovering on the edge
Of a perilous precipice.

Arjuna returns to question Lord Krishna once more.

36 The armies stand stock still,
Amazed,
Awe struck
By Krishna's presence
And of his addressing Arjuna.
They await silently
For the battle to begin,
If at all.
Who knows
What fate destiny has in store?
Oh, Krishna,
What drives a man to wickedness
Even against his wishes
As if compelled by the Gods themselves?

This is a great moral dilemma, which differs from the conditioned thought patterns of conventional morality. What happens when we are told we can do what we like, as all actions are God's, not ours? In fact, our right conditioning protects us, along with God's will. There is nothing to fear.

37   It is desire
       And anger
       Born of passion
       And craving,
       Both are blind and wicked,
       They are your enemies.

Here the concept of the Gunas or Qualities is introduced.
Passion is Rajas – a hyper-activity. Tamas is the opposite, a
dull passivity or inertia. Sattva is the clear light of intellectual and emotional balance, lucid clarity. Ramana advocated
a vegetarian diet with milk products as the best aid to Sattva.
Rajas is encouraged by meat, spices, and alcohol, Tamas by a
stale, junk food diet. This theme will be extensively expanded
as the great teaching is revealed by Krishna.

38   Fire is hidden by
       Smoke.
       Mirrors are hidden
       By dust.
       Like a baby covered
       In the mother's womb
       This teaching is hidden
       Like that.

This is a cryptic verse. The teaching is an open secret but
veiled to those who lack the receptivity to understand its
meaning.

39   Knowledge is blackened
       By the desires
       Hungry after sensual gratification.

The Gita does not condemn natural inclinations but *excessive passions*, which can destroy an individual if allowed too much rein. Balanced harmony is the theme. All is included, but there are guidelines and sign posts for Sattvic behavior. Forced control or repression of feelings can lead to undesirable side effects. Most of those on this Way of the Householder were married. Ramana Maharshi said: "Married or unmarried, a man can realize the Self."

40 The six senses,
The laid down patterns
Of conditioned thought,
The dubious gift of intellect,
Make up the House of Excessive Desires,
Obscuring wisdom.
The seeker is sorely deluded.

41 So, Arjuna,
Watch, witness your senses
In action,
Then you shall learn
How to ignore the destroyer
Of Self-knowledge.
This is the way to their destruction.

42 Mighty are the senses,
Mighty are the thoughts,
Mighty the conceptual
Intellect
But much mightier still
Is the Source,

The Creator Godhead,
The Self, Consciousness, Awareness, Peace.

43 So know thy Self,
Consciousness, Awareness,
"Isness," Peace,
Beyond the mind.
Let thy Self
Master the self.
Slay the enemy!
Of excessive desires,
Hard though it seems.

IV

The way of
self-knowledge

1   I taught this High Teaching
     To the Sun God
     And His Son,
     Founder of the Human Race
     And his Son
     Founder King of our Dynasty.

The Lord Krishna as an Avatar or messenger from the Divine
Source tells Arjuna that He as Consciousness, Awareness,
Self, Godhead, Peace had informed Vivasvan, The Sun God,
of this teaching. This verse places Krishna at the cosmological level as a Divine Force affecting the destiny of our
solar system. Manu was the founder of the human race by
Vedic tradition. The Laws of Manu were the legal code of
the Vedic civilization. No less a philosopher than Frederick

Neitzsche believed them to be superior to the laws of Moses although there are many parallels. Manu's son, Iksvaku, became the founder of a line of Solar Kings ruling the Vedic civilization in the times of the Ancient Rishis who revealed the truth of the Vedas and the Upanishads. Historically, Krishna was a king referred to in the Upanishads. Like Jesus and the Buddha, the Gita uses an historical figure as well as a Divine Teacher to guide humanity. All were of royal descent. Krishna is referred to in the Chandogya Upanishad (III.17.6) as a pupil of Ghora Angirasa, a priest of the Sun.

2   It was handed down
     By tradition,
     Passed on by word of mouth
     From master to pupil.
     The royal sages knew it,
     But it has been buried,
     By the sands of time.

3   Today this
     Ancient supreme secret
     I give to you,
     Because you are my beloved
     Devotee and friend.

4   Arjuna questioned:
     But, Krishna,
     You were born after
     The Sun God,
     How am I to understand
     That you taught him?

5 Many births of mine
Have happened
And of yours too.
I know them all,
You do not.

The transmigration of the subtle body takes place after death when it returns to the pool, or Source of Consciousness. Consciousness creates new bodies from different components and aggregates to enter the Lila or divine drama at any chosen moment. This explains child prodigies who are born with talents already formed, eg Mozart and Mendelssohn. Ramana Maharshi said he *never did any spiritual practice*. His Self-Realization was the consequence of a previous life. He never said his previous life.

6 Unborn and Eternal
Consciousness, the Self, I am,
Lord of Creation
I am.
Yet re-sourcing
From my own nature
I take birth through
My own power.

7 Whenever righteousness
Decays and rots, like stinking fish,
And unrighteousness
Prevails, like disgusting dung
I come.

Divine Power always upholds the planetary balance. Ramana Maharshi was active at the worst moment in human history – two dreadful world wars, the holocaust and the atom bomb.

8   For upholding the sincere,
     For the destruction of
     The foolish,
     For the re-establishment
     Of righteousness,
     I appear from age to age
     In different forms.
     The wise recognize me
     When I come.

9   He who correctly
     Understands my divinity
     And activity
     Is not to suffer a
     Reincarnation
     But returns to the Source.

Reincarnation is not exactly the same as transmigration. It is a lesser doctrine suggesting that where there is ignorance the foolish one will have to suffer again until he awakes. It has become a popular belief. Only the subtle body can transmigrate. The brain, holding the egotistic identity decomposes with the body. This is a mystery the rational mind cannot follow. Reincarnation is part of the exoteric tradition. By performing "good deeds" men and women believe they will have a better life next time. The Gita contains the esoteric doctrine (*para vidya*) as well as the exoteric (*apara vidya*), the lower and higher doctrine. We have to discriminate between the two and more towards the "para vidya." Reincarnation satisfies many who feel there is injustice in some born crippled beggars while others are healthy, wealthy, and wise. But happiness is within, through the will to accept and affirm "what is." Many a millionaire is miserable and paranoid. Many a lame beggar is serenely content.

10   Very many have been born
Who, freed from cares
And attachment,
Fear, boredom, and horrific
Anger,
Become totally absorbed
In the One,
Their own Self
Immanent in all.
Then resting in the Heart
Take refuge there.
One becomes purified
By the astringent austerity
Of this teaching.
They then join me in my state
Of Self-Realization.

By "wisdom" the Gita means "Self-knowledge" or jnana – this was affirmed in the West by Socrates and Plato, and in the East, From Dakshinarmurti, Gaudapada, Shankara, Jnanashewara, the Buddha, Ramakrishna, Ramana Maharshi, and Vivekananda. Krishna is fundamental to all these sages

as is the Gita. Enlightenment is a virus you may catch by
association with sages and familiarity with their works.
Association with the wise – satsang – works by osmosis.

11   Whichever way seekers
      Arrive at the One,
      Like homing pigeons,
      Flying their own path,
      Never colliding,
      I come to them
      Embracing them wholeheartedly
      In love,
      If they will only open to me.
      All their different ways
      Are only ways to Me.

The two wings of the bird on which to fly home are surrender and Self-inquiry.

12   Of course – naturally,
      Those fools and idiots
      Desiring success and security
      Pray to and worship various gods.
      Often their wishes are
      Quickly answered.
      I am generous.
      All who approach me
      Sincerely from the bottom of their hearts
      And seek God and Me as their refuge
      I accept

From mercy and compassion and love.
After all, I am them and they are Me,
All I assure you will be well,
Very, very well.

13   The structure of society
Is preordained
Accept "what is"
Wholeheartedly
But not necessarily with
Approval.
In this Dark Age of the Kali Yuga.
Society is based
On men's Qualities
Yet as their Source
I remain inactive
And unchangeable.

14   Actions neither affect
Me nor infect me
I am immune from these
Fleas which carry plague.
Nor do I desire
To revel in eating the
Luscious fruits
Of success.
He who understands this of Me,
The core of his own being,
His Real Self
Is also like Me, free.

15   Safe in the knowledge
     Taught by ancient sages
     Who sought freedom
     And yet remained
     Engaged in Action,
     So do this also, Arjuna!

16   What is action and
     Inaction?
     Even the wise
     Become confused
     Alas, alas.
     My explanation
     Shall free you
     From this dilemma.

17   The difference
     Has to be understood,
     Between action
     And inaction.
     This is hard.

18   He alone is wise
     Who has ended
     Questioning
     About action or inaction.
     Who can see inaction
     In action
     And action in inaction
     Is wise.

19 One, whose endeavors,
And desires
Are free from motive and
Their consequences,
And therefore purified,
By the sacred fire of
Wisdom,
Is a sage.

20 Totally indifferent
To the luscious tempting plums
Of success,
Ever happy and free
He is "not doing"
While it appears
He is.
Oh mystery of mysteries.
Fathom this,
Arjuna, and you will be freed.

21 One who acts with
Body alone,
Desireless,
Resting in the Heart,
Thought free,
Having renounced
Possessiveness,
Can do no harm.

The Heart is often used as a synonym for the Self. Ramana

Maharshi said that from his own experience, the spiritual
Heart, not the fleshy one, was on the right side of the chest.
It was a point on which one could focus attention. This led
to removing identification with the outside world as well as
opening up a gateway to the Self. The laser beam of attention, passing from the chakra between the eyebrows into the
Heart could lead to a palpitation on this right side (spurana)
and eventual absorption of the mind into the Heart.

22   Delighted,
      Welcoming,
      Whatever comes
      Unsought.
      Beyond the psychic
      Opposites
      Free from envy
      Equal in success
      Or failure
      He is not bound by deeds.

23   The deeds of whoever
      Is non-attached,
      Free,
      Whose mind is firm in
      Wisdom,
      Whose actions are an
      Offering to Self,
      The Source of his being,
      Immanent in his Heart,
      And transcendent,
      As the Godhead,

Are completely dissolved.
Like a dew drop
That slips into the sea.

24 The deed of offering
Is to Brahman
And is Brahman.
The sacred fire is Brahman,
The offerer is Brahman.
By acting with mind
Fixed on Brahman
A man becomes Brahman.

Brahman here is another synonym for Consciousness, Awareness, Self, Godhead, Peace, Source of Creation, and "Isness."

25 Some make sacrifices
To outer Gods
Others offer their egotism
In the bonfire of Consciousness.

26 Some offer their senses
In the flames of restraint.
Some offer the objects
Of sensuality
In the same fire.

27 Some offer sensuality,
Fuelled by their vitality,

On the funeral pyre
Kindled by the stick of
Wisdom.

28   Some swear vows,
Give away their goods,
Practice austerity,
Even their learning
And knowledge.

29   Some to restrain
The wild horses
Of the mind
Practice breath control,
Watching or retaining the flow
Of exhalation and inhalation.

Ramana Maharshi advocated watching the flow of breath as an aid to quieten the mind. For those who cannot sleep at night because of nagging thoughts, watching the flow of breath is a great aid.

30   Some watch their diet,
Eating only fresh foods,
Offer their life breath
Into the life breath.
All these understand
The meaning
Of "offering"
And avoid wrong deeds.

The life breath is the Sacred Prajna. The powerful primal life force in the subtle energy of the air we breathe.

31   These who enjoy
       The sacred leavings
       After the "offering"
       Reach Brahman.
       There is no success
       For those who fail to
       Make their life an "offering,"
       Either in this world
       Or any other.

32   All forms of austerity
       Advised in scripture
       Derive from action.
       Knowing this you will
       Find freedom.

33   But the highest
       Of all "offerings"
       Is the one known
       Through Wisdom.
       All deeds end in Wisdom.

34   Reach this knowledge
       By loving your teacher,
       By questioning him
       And giving him or her service.
       The wise who know

The Truth
Will teach you this knowledge.

To find a teacher or guru (dispeller of darkness) with whom
you resonate is an important step on this path.

35   Know this and you
       Will never sink
       Into the quick sands
       Of confusion.
       Through this knowledge
       You will see
       All beings in the Self,
       Sharing the same
       Consciousness, Awareness, Godhead,
       As with Me.

36   Even if you were the king
       Of ignorant fools
       You will cross over the
       Fast flowing river
       Of worldliness
       On this raft of knowledge.

37   As a roaring fire
       Eats its wood,
       So, the fire of knowledge
       Reduces the false
       Sense of "I am the Doer"
       To ashes.

38 Knowledge is the
Greatest purifier.
Just as clear
Crystal fountain water
Cleans all around it.
One who is grounded in
Wisdom
Finds in course of time
His own Self for himself.

39 One who has great faith
And power of concentrated
Attention,
Like a laser beam,
Cuts through dense metal.
So controlling sensuality
He finds Self-knowledge
And he swiftly enjoys
Great peace.

40 One sunk in ignorance,
Faithless and constantly
In doubt,
Is miserable in this life,
And any other life beyond.

41 He who has surrendered
His false sense of "I am the Doer,"
Imagining he is the author
Of his deeds,

Who has conquered doubt
By certainty,
Who is Self-possessed,
Is never bound by
Any deeds
He may be forced to
Perform by destiny.

42   So Arjuna, armed
With this mighty sword
Of true knowledge,
Cut down the weeds of doubt
That crowd in your heart.
Be bold!
Stand firm in Truth,
Wake up!
Wake up!

V

Renunciation of the fruits of deeds

Lord Krishna's powers held the two armies in still silence while he continued to teach Arjuna, who then questioned him.

1   Krishna,
    You seem to praise
    Giving up action
    As well as action itself.
    Which is better?

Krishna replied:

2   They both lead to
    The same end

But of the two,
Right action is better.

3   He is a constant
Renunciate
Who neither desires
Nor hates.
Freed from these terrible
Demon opposites
He is simply released
From bondage.

4   It is child's babble
Not the words of a sage
That the path of knowledge
And action differ.
He who stands firm in both
Receives their benefits.

The ways of Karma Yoga (action) and Jnana Yoga (knowledge) are essentially the same in the end. All the yogas including Bhakti (devotion) overlap leading to the destruction of the false "ego."

5   Men of Knowledge,
Men of Action,
Can reach the same
Understanding.
He who sees the two paths
As one, sees correctly.

6   Yet it is hard to reach
      Renunciation
      Without the wisdom
      Born of action.
      A sage who knows this
      Finds the Self of Consciousness, Awareness,
          Peace.

7   He whose mind is cleansed,
      As a river runs through stables,
      By the wisdom of action,
      And controls his sensuality,
      And knows his own Self,
      To be one with the Self of all,
      As Consciousness, Awareness,
      Peace, Godhead,
      Is unaffected even when performing difficult
          deeds.

8–9   Arjuna, listen carefully
      With attention.
      He who knows the real truth
      Knows he is not "the
      Doer" of anything.
      Whether seeing mountain ranges,
      Or dung heaps,
      Hearing sweet music or
      The din of the city,
      While touching
      Deer skins or porcupines,
      Smelling sandalwood,

Incense, or rotting corpses,
Eating fine, fresh rice and samba,
Or stale crusts of nan,
Walking in the green forest
Or village rubbish tip,
Sleeping soundly without dreams
Or badly with hideous nightmares,
Breathing fresh air from the
Ocean or smog with a
Blocked nose,
Reciting fine mystical
Poetry or babbling childish
Prattle,
Releasing the golden river
Of urinology,
Or hard sheep shit,
Receiving unexpected gifts
Or rejecting events violently,
Opening the eyes to see
The world dream or closing
The eyes and destroying it
At one fell swoop.
He truly knows only his
God given senses,
That top forepart of his brain,
Contemplating their
Objects,
Which are not what they seem
But must be accepted.

The Gita psychology emphasizes the power of the senses and urges that they be understood to be restrained.

10   That lucky man or woman
Who surrenders their identification
To anything or any body-mind
Especially their own,
Resigns all his or her deeds
To the Godhead, Self, Source,
Consciousness, Awareness, Peace,
And remains untouched
As does the pink lotus flower
Floating serenely on a blue lake.

Ramakrishna wrote: "He who comes to know that he is only an instrument in the hands of the Lord has no egotistic feeling."

11   Ending the vile disease of
Attachment,
Sages engage in action
With the body.
The bundle of thought patterns,
The power of reason,
The six senses,
Intuitions from the Self,
Through the subtle body
And her feelings,
For one aim only,
Purification.

Many modern people do not approve of the corrupt over materialistic society by which we have been conditioned. Every "enterprise" wishes to make more and more money in order to survive in the competitive jungle. Advertisers and companies exploit sex, alcoholism, desire for more goods, and hedonistic pleasure as the means. Football mania, celebrities trash TV are the bitch Goddesses fawning at the feet of the golden calf. Lord Krishna, as an Avatar promises to restore the Dharma of Righteous Harmony and once again we may see a golden cultural age such as happened in Vedic India, Ancient Greece, Renaissance Italy, sixteenth-century England, seventeenth-century Holland and nineteenth-century Germany.

Dumbing down to the popular level may bring in money but not culture. Culture comes when a genius sweeps clean the century and sets a new form or style – in music, Beethoven in the nineteenth century; in poetry, T. S. Eliot in the twentieth-century. In painting, Rene Magritte, who foreshadows a new metaphysical painting yet to be widely practiced. In philosophy we have Schopenhauer who linked the Upanishadic wisdom to mainstream Western philosophy and Nietzsche a super-critic of culture who affirmed the Laws of Manu as preferable to a "rigged democracy." J. Krishnamurti said we live in a corrupt society. Awakening, by more men and women through the advanced Gita teaching will restore the Dharma. Ramakrishna, Parahamsa, Ramana Maharshi, and Aurobindo were such pioneers for a new age.

12–13   The Self-controlled
        Who has sacrificed
        The idea of "I am the Doer"
        Lives easily at peace

In the City of Nine Gates,
This body,
Neither acting him
Nor making anyone else to act.

According to the great Katha Upanishad (Upanishad means mystical teaching), a clearly Advaitic scripture, the nine gates of our Body City are two eyes, two ears, the nose, the mouth, the two internal organs of excretion and the one of generation. This is also discussed in another late Upanishad of an Advaitic nature, the Svetasvatara III.18.

The Katha says: "The Self-existent made the senses turn outward. Accordingly, man looks toward what is without, and sees not what is within. Rare is he who, longing for freedom, shuts his eyes to what is outside and beholds the Self."[1]

14   The Supreme Self,
Absolute Consciousness,
Impersonal Awareness,
Godhead,
Source,
Peace,
Creates
Neither a "doer"
Nor "doing"
Nor unites deeds
With their fruits.
It is one's own

---

[1] Christopher Isherwood's translation.

Pre-ordained destiny
Alone, which is the "Doer."

15   The Self,
      Absolute Consciousness,
      Awareness,
      Peace,
      Godhead,
      Does not take sides
      Either with man's goodness
      Or darkness.
      Wisdom is veiled by ignorance.
      So men are gravely
      Deluded.
      Thank your stars for Grace,
      Arjuna,
      You are with Me
      A hero on the side of righteousness
      And not sunk in evil
      Like some sewer rat.

16   In those sunk
      In the gross body,
      Their basic ignorance
      Can be destroyed by words
      Which, like the blazing
      Noon-day sun,
      Reveal the Supreme.

17   If your attention

Is firmly fixed
On your Awareness,
Consciousness, Self, Source,
Peace, Sense of Spaciousness,
Silence of the Heart,
Merge in that.
Pointing and devoted to "That"
Then ignorance dissolves
Like a salt doll falling into the
Sea of Grace.
By wisdom you are freed,
Who knows to where?
Or who cares to where?
There is no going back,
So, dear friend, beware,
Be aware.

18   The sage sees
With an equal eye
A scholastic Brahmin
Or a humble illiterate,
A cow, symbol of Brahman's gifts,
An elephant, symbol of Ganesha,
Remover of all obstacles,
The dog, a humanized wolf,
A cat, a humanized tiger in
Miniature,
Or the beggar,
That it is the duty
Of society to help

Back into true manhood
Or womanhood.

The problem of beggars and outcasts is severe. What can one do? The Lord ordained their poverty. Many are happier in their way of life than millionaires. They have opted out of a corrupt and pressurized society. The late Robert Adams,[2] the American sage, told me he was openhearted to all beggars, this is their Karma, so if you want to understand compassion start with him. But there is a problem. Some are professionals and use the money for alcohol and drugs. So Ramesh says have plenty of small change; a dime is worth more to a beggar than it is to a well-heeled citizen. This is again an inscrutable mystery of Source. We must recall that Ramana Maharshi in his early days begged from door to door for sustenance. Who are we to judge the inscrutable?

19   In this life of delusions
      Those who are equi-poised
      Have conquered the
      Problems of existence.
      Flawless and uniform is
      Consciousness, Awareness, God, Spaciousness,
          Self, Peace, Source,
      So in That they are firmly established.

20   The knower of Consciousness, the Self,
      Established in Spaciousness and God,
      Steadfast
      In clarity.

[2] *Silence of the Heart*, Acropolis Books, Atlanta, Georgia.

Neither rejoices over pleasant
Happenings
Nor regrets bitter
Disappointments.

21   Not over involved with
Outer events
He finds happiness in
His Self, Consciousness, Awareness,
Godhead, Peace,
United with his own Source of Being.
He then enjoys endless peace.

22   The pigsty of the senses
Is utter misery,
They are all changing endlessly.
A wise man shuns their obscenity.

23   He who before dying
Can resist desire and anger
Is integrated and happy.

24   That man whose
Happiness is inside
Not in outer baubles,
Whose joy and light
Are also inward,
Reaches Perfect Peace
And is Peace.

25   Those who reach Perfect Peace,
       Whose flaws and blemishes
       Are destroyed by Grace,
       No longer have a
       Sense of separation.
       Thoughts are controlled,
       And they only wish for
       The well being of all
       Their fellow creatures.

26   Perfect Peace is
       Palpable
       And like deep silence
       Can be felt by those
       Freed from the dread tyranny
       Of anger and desire.
       Who have subdued
       Their arrogant, wandering,
       Perverted minds,
       And have touched the Self
       Of Absolute Consciousness,
       The Godhead hiding in the Heart.

27–28 The sage
       Earnest for freedom
       Has conquered desire,
       Fear, and wrath,
       Turning away from
       Glitzy spectacles
       And sits with gaze

Fixed between his
Eyebrows
And watches
His life breath
Flow freely.

The Gita gives a pointer to mind control. Fixing the attention on the chakra between the eyebrows (the pineal gland) stills the mind, as does watching the flow of breath without interference. These are techniques of Raja Yoga. The best guide to its practice and theory is Vivekananda or Swami Sivananda.[3]

29 Knowing me as
Self,
Absolute Consciousness,
Peace, Awareness,
Godhead,
I am the enjoyer
Of sacrifice
Offering an astringent austerity,
The ruler of all worlds,
The friend of all beings,
One shall know Perfect Peace.

[3] Divine Life Society, with centers worldwide.

VI

Meditation

1   He is a true
    Renunciate
    Who performs his duty
    Regardless of expectation,
    Profit, or result.
    It is not enough
    Merely to renounce the
    Fire ceremony and
    Business of the average
    Householder.

2   That which is
    Called Renunciation

Is Yoga.
None becomes a
Yogi
Without renouncing
Gross desires,
Ambitions,
And fantasy.

3   For the wise, silent one,
Moving towards Yoga,
Action is said to be the
Way,
After touching the Self,
Peace,
And stillness is the way.

4   When a man or woman
Is unattached
To their sensuality
And to their deeds
And has renounced
All desire for name
And fame
They have reached Yoga.

5   Let men and women
Raise themselves,
Let them not debase
Themselves
For his or her Self

Is the Friend,
The ego his foe.

6 To him who has
Subdued his ego
By the Self of
Absolute Consciousness, Source
Awareness, Peace, Godhead,
This Self is a great friend.
But to the one who has
Not yet subdued his Ego
The Self remains like a
Tiger, his jaws wide open.
Ego's head is in the
Tiger's mouth.
It can rest assured
That it will be subdued
Sooner or later.

7 To one whose ego
Has been subdued
The Self is equi-poised,
Whether in the noonday
Sun of the burning desert
Or the half-moon night of
The frozen Arctic waste.
Similarly, in honor
When all praise,
And disgrace when all blame.

8   Integration
     Is
     When the Yogi is
     Happy
     Through knowledge and wisdom,
     Unshakeable,
     Master of the senses.
     He who can see
     A brown clod of earth,
     A gray stone on the beach,
     A yellow nugget of gold,
     As essentially made
     Of the same stuff
     Is a Yogi.

Modern science has shown that matter is an arrangement
of atoms, molecules, and electrons held in a force-field of
consciousness for a specific time. In ancient times matter was
seen as an arrangement of elements (fire, earth, ether, water)
in a similar way. Modern science equates with the wisdom of
the Vedas in many ways. Fritjof Capra points this out in the
Tao of Physics and other works.

9   Lord is he who looks
     With equal eye
     On the well-wisher,
     The amiable friend,
     The hostile foe.
     The alienated from God,
     The related to God,

The righteous
And unrighteous.
He is clear and unattached.

10   Alone in solitude
The Yogi meditates
In his body, watching, wandering
Thoughts,
Impartially,
Still,
Desireless,
The sense of possession at rest.

11   He assumes a
Firm posture
In a place of sheer beauty
And delight,
Neither too high
Nor too low,
He sits
On sacred grass.
And a deer-skin.

12   Seated,
With attention collected
Thoughts and senses
Checked,
He empties his mind
Of thought.

13   Body,
     Head,
     Spine erect
     Tall as an oak tree,
     Feeling wide
     As the spacious
     Firmament,
     He rests his attention
     Sensing the tip of his
     Nose.

This way the flow of breath may be witnessed, stilling the mind.

14   Quiet,
     Fearless,
     Impartially
     Watching what comes up,
     Or inquiring
     Into the Self.
     Mind subdued
     Celibate in mind,
     Firmly
     Integrated.

Celibacy is traditionally an aid to Self-Realization amongst monastic orders. Retention of the semen (ojas) was thought to bring special powers. However, most Vedic royalty and warriors, merchants and servants were married. Ramana Maharshi proclaimed "married or unmarried a man (or woman) can realize the Self. There is no sex in the Self. It is a consequence of identification with the mind body organism." Most of his close disciples, Self-Realized through him were married. Most modern teachers of Advaita-Vedanta are married. Nothing need be suppressed. Most spiritual practice injunctions are pointers. There is no "having to do anything." If spontaneously a wish arises to perform a particular practice, this is fine, the will of the Source. Forcing a practice never works. Relaxed energy is the key to effort.

15   So at-one-ment,
The Yoga of subdued mind,
Reaches the understanding
Of Self, Consciousness,
Godhead, Awareness, Peace,
Source.
Essentially innermost in
Him
And transcendental in
Krishna
When he personifies the Divine
Cosmic force.

Krishna may be seen as the projection of the core of Arjuna's own inner Self or being.

16   Yoga is not for one
Who is a glutton,
Or fasts overmuch,
Nor for one who
Oversleeps too much
Or stays up too long.

The Yoga in this chapter is the middle way, as the Buddha
taught harmonious balance between sensual excess and vig-
orous asceticism.

17   For a Yogi
      Who is moderate
      In eating, resting,
      Sleeping, waking,
      In all his deeds,
      Soon becomes the destroyer
      Of suffering.

18   When the subdued mind
      Rests in the Heart,
      Alone,
      Desireless,
      Then one is integrated.

19   As a tallow lamp
      In a windless glade
      Never flickers,
      So is the Yogi
      Who with collected
      Attention
      Inquires into the
      Nature of the Self, Absolute
      Consciousness, Peace, Godhead,
      Awareness. Silence,
      Peace,
      Source of his own Being.

20 When the bird's nest
    Of thoughts
    Is quietened by meditation
    And reaches stillness
    And silence,
    Then perceiving the Self of
    Absolute Consciousness,
    Peace, Awareness, Godhead,
    Even in the ordinary
    Everyday
    Egotistic conceptual mind,
    One is very, very happy,
    Resting in That.

21 When one knows
    That Peace
    Felt by the intellectual
    Understanding
    Beyond the senses,
    Firm in that,
    One never moves away from
    This Reality.

22 When reaching an understanding
    Experientially
    Of what the Self is
    As your Consciousness, Awareness, Peace.
    There is nothing left
    Deeper to gain.
    Once established,

One is never moved,
Even by the tragic grief
Of sudden death
When a close loved one dies.

23   Then one realizes
The separation from this
Grief
Is union or Yoga.
Persevere with
A positive, affirming
Attitude, Arjuna!
Do not grieve!

C. J. Jung said that "angst" or existential grief was the disease
of modern man, only to be cured by a return to the Self or
Individuation as he called it.

24–25   Renouncing all
Fantastic desires
Born of flaming ambition
And then restraining
The senses
By collected attention
At every window of perception
One slowly reaches peace.
The intellect is held still
Resting in the Heart
Allowing no random stream
Of thoughts
To meander and disturb.

26   However,
      The restless, rude,
      Unruly monkey mind
      Rebels mischievously
      Like a naughty schoolboy,
      Impishly insolent.
      One reins it in
      And returns to the Self.

27   To such a meditation,
      Calm, blue, cool,
      Tranquil as a mountain lake
      Beneath a windless sky,
      Free
      From the bubonic plague
      Of passions,
      One with the Self–Absolute
      Consciousness, Awareness,
      Godhead, Peace.
      Then enters the bridegroom,
      The Supreme.

28   Those held in
      Yogic meditation
      Are free from error,
      Striking the mark.
      With the arrow of attention
      They gracefully
      Arrive at Peace
      And Self-Recognition.

29   One who is
      Gladly integrated in That,
      Sees all with equal eye,
      Seeing his Self in all
      And All in his Self.

This equates with Jesus' injunction to "love thy neighbor as
thy Self."

30   One who knows Me
      As the Self everywhere,
      The seer – the seeing and
      the seen, are in Me as Godhead
      Manifested
      And all are embraced in My Space
      As That,
      I shall never ever lose
      Him,
      As a father loves
      His child.
      Nor will he ever lose Me.
      Rest assured.

31   That Yogi
      Firm in his Oneness,
      His Consciousness, Awareness,
      Which is God,
      Worships Me as the
      Personification of That
      Immanent in his Heart.

In all beings That
Dwells in Me
Though performing
Innumerable deeds.

32   He who sees all
Impartially,
Non-judgmentally,
With an equal eye
And bears the pleasures
And pains
Of his fellow creatures
As if his own
Is approaching perfection.

Arjuna is now moved to question his teacher, Krishna.

33–34   This Yoga of Equanimity
Seems to me to be
Unfirm and unlasting
Because the mischievous
Monkey mind
Is wild and restless
Like the wind.

35   I agree, Arjuna.
The mind is hard
To control
And restless.
Yoga is not easy to master

Yet there are ways
Of meditation and dispassion.

36   So, Arjuna
For the poor being,
Who lacks any self-control,
Yoga is hard to master
But there are ways, indeed.

37   Arjuna.
Tell me Lord Krishna
What happens to he who has faith
But no control
And whose perverted mind wanders away
Without reaching perfection
In Yoga?

38   Fallen
From Earth and Heaven,
Doesn't he die
Like a cloud split
In two
By forked lightning,
Unsupported, abandoned,
On the way to
Recover his own true Self?

39   Banish this doubt
Oh Krishna
I implore you!

Just as you would
Exile
A child rapist
From the midst of
Your city.

What follows is a cherished compassionate passage of great hope which points to the way of surrender for those who find the way of Raja Yoga, Pranayama, Meditation, and Self-inquiry much too difficult.

40   I vow, Arjuna,
Neither in this world
Or any other
Will he ever be
Destroyed.
No one who is intent
On finding
Righteousness
Ever comes to ultimate grief!

This is consolation for those who believe they are a continuous egotistic entity progressing or failing from life to life. In fact, this is encouragement to the miserable seeker. There is no egotistic entity in fact. This mistake that "I am the Doer" notion is the source of all suffering.

41   Having reached the
Heavenly state of sainthood
And lived there for years,
Then he who falls from Yoga

Is transmigrated
In his subtle body
To a noble and auspicious
Family.

42　Or better still
His subtle body may transmigrate
To a family
Of wise Sages.
Such a situation is very
Rare indeed.

It is worth noting that Papaji, a foremost disciple of Ramana Maharshi, whose messengers are now active in the West teaching the Advarta Philosophy, was in fact a nephew of Sri Rama Thirta, an acknowledged Jnani, in India. Ramana Maharshi said he never did any spiritual practice or Sadhama. His early Self-Realization must have been the result of a (not his) previous life. He was born into an educated Brahmin family. Robert Adams, the late American sage, another disciple, realized at a very early age, before meeting Ramana.

The teaching is rigorous but necessary to shift the seeker over the brink into the abyss of no-thing-ness and inner freedom.

VII

The way of
joyful wisdom

1 Now pay close attention, Arjuna.
Listen!
I shall tell you how,
With your attention focused on Me
As the Sat-Guru in your Heart
Your Self as Awareness, Godhead,
Peace, Consciousness
Immanent and transcendent,
And taking refuge in Me,
Meditating on Me,
You shall know Me
In full,
My attributes,
And my essence,

Which are you, your Self,
I promise.

2   I shall teach
     Both the fundamental
     And detailed wisdom.
     If you understood that,
     Nothing more ever needs
     To be known.

The Gita now moves from the first necessary step of spiritual
practice based on Raja Yoga to the advanced stage of knowledge – Wisdom, Jnana, or the Ultimate Understanding.

3   Out of thousands seeking
     Perhaps only one
     Knows me
     As I truly, really, really am.

This echoes "many are called but few are chosen" in
Christianity. In terms of Advaita Vedanta, Self-Realization
comes from whom the Atman-Brahaman chooses through
Grace, after the intellectual understanding descends into the
Heart. Trying to "get" Realization is an impediment. It is
better to call off the search and wait patiently, meanwhile
affirming life as it is offered.

4   The elements
     Of dark, rich brown, earth,
     Clear, blue-green water,
     Roaring red fire,

The mysterious heavenly unknown, invisible,
   transparent ether,
The live potent force of air,
Call.
And the beautifully wired
Transistor – neuron – personal computer brain
Termed intellect,
These are the divisions of my
Nature.

We are introduced to the concept of Prakriti, which means the Force of Nature, in Western terms, in the sense of its apparent manifestation. This is fully discussed by Arthur Schopenhauer in his book *On the Will in Nature*. As a student of the Upanishads, Schopenhauer's work is recommended to those of intellectual bent.

5   This is my lower Nature,
    The technicolored beauty,
    Red, blue, yellow, and all its permutations
    You see through the senses.
    My higher Nature is
    The Life Force or the Will
    Of God, the Source, Consciousness,
    The Numinon and
    The substratum
    By which the whole universe
    Is upheld.

The lower Prakriti or Nature is the universal energy-field of the quantum physicists. The analogy of the "field" is to be enlarged in a later chapter (XIII).

6   All beings
     Are born
     Of this dual Nature,
     An arrangement in Consciousness,
     A dance of atoms and elements,
     However described.
     I am that I am
     Is the origin of the
     Universe
     And its dissolution.

Atomic theory was known to the ancient world. It is referred to in the Upanishads and in Ancient Greece proposed by Heraclitus. It is a miracle that the ancients perceived the atomic world without the aid of electron microscopes, and astrological knowledge without telescopes. Krishna now speaks as an Avadhuta or Avatar, a representative of the Divine Voice addressing humanity. "I am that I am" was the response the God gave to Moses when he inquired about the divine identity.

7   There is nothing above me
     All is living
     Like a network of jewels
     On a thread.

Ramesh Balsekar uses this analogy in his seminal book, *A Net of Jewels,*[1] which contains this contemporary Mumbai sage's best aphorisms selected by his disciple, Wayne Liquorman, for daily meditation.

[1] Advaita Press USA.

8　I am the primal blue water lily
　　Floating in clear lustrous waters,
　　The shining silvery Grace
　　Of the radiant moon,
　　The burnished gold of
　　The blazing sun.
　　The sacred chant of Aum in
　　The revealed Rig Veda,
　　The electric current that
　　Throbs through the ether,
　　And the strength
　　Inherent in Man's seed.

Aum is the primeval sound from which Creation emanated.
It is fully discussed in the *Mundakya Upanishad*.

9　The healthy sweet smell of
　　The damp Earth
　　And the red, crackling blaze of fire,
　　The transparent vital air
　　Moving all that moves,
　　The holiness of hallowed souls,
　　The undying root, Brahman,
　　From which all has sprung,
　　All that Is.

10　The wisdom of the wise,
　　The intelligence of the learned,
　　The genius of the great,
　　The radiant splendor of the
　　Splendid,

The leonine strength of the brave
When free from desire and craving,
The light of the illustrious.

11   The tiger's strength of
      The bold, am I,
      When free from desire
      And craving.
      I am true desire,
      Not in conflict
      With righteousness.

12   Whatever mind-states
      Arise from the Qualities
      Whose exuberant play
      Holds the Universe in balance,
      Clear and inward,
      Active and outward,
      Dark and downward,
      I transcend them all.
      They come from me
      But I am not contained in them.

Here we are introduced to the three Gunas, active, passive, and neutralizing forces, or Raja, Tamas, and Sattva, which are the perceptive psychological insights into the basis of mental states. They are described fully in Chapter XVII. The Gurdjieff teaching also endorses this insight of the three forces.[2]

---

[2] See psychological commentaries in *Gurdjieff's Teaching* by Maurice Nicol (three volumes).

13 The world
    Deluded
    By these three forces
    Is ignorant
    Of My Presence,
    Transcendent,
    Unchanging.

14 This is my Divine
    Hypnosis,
    Maya.
    It is hard to see through,
    Only those who totally surrender
    Penetrate this illusion.

We are now introduced to the great philosophical truth of Maya or world illusion. Briefly stated, the world is a representation created by the *senses* and interpreted by the intellect. Nothing is really what it appears to seem, it is unsubstantial, unreal, and dream like. The world is an appearance in consciousness. I am the space for events to happen in at many different levels. What things are in themselves is a mystery. We can say they are in a state of flux or objects in process. Time and space are "a priori" concepts in the brain, which provide the framework for the world moving picture to proceed. This is eloquently described by Kant and Schopenhauer.[3] Causality is another inborn concept (ie cause and effect relationship). This makes man superior to the ani-

[3] See Arthur Schopenhauer, *World as Will and Representation*, Dover Publications Inc, 1966 or Immanuel Kant, *Critique of Pure Reason*, for a fuller explanation.

mal because he possesses the power of conceptual reasoning
as a consequence.

15   Those hostile to the
Way of righteous harmony,
The basest of mankind,
Their minds confused
By the divine hypnosis,
Are demonic,
They are not interested
In truth and oppose it,
Often vigorously
If they feel threatened by it.

16   Seekers
Are of four types:
Those who suffer,
Those who need knowledge,
Those who wish to
Gain powers.
And the wise.

17   The best are the wise ones,
Steadfast and devoted,
Beloved I am of them
And they to me.

18   All seekers are noble
But the sage is as my Self,
Integrated,

He is established
In Me as the Supreme.

Lord Krishna's personification of himself as Consciousness
Absolute, Awareness, Self, Source, Peace, and Godhead has a
powerful resonance, unique in mystical poetry.

19   After many transmigrations
      Of their subtle bodies
      The men of wisdom come to me
      Realizing I am the All,
      Such great souls are very rare.

This is a major hint of non-dualism or Advaita, seeing
Krishna as the All (Vasudeva), which will be expanded as the
poem progresses.

20   But those whose knowledge
      Is clouded by desire
      Resort to false Gods
      And practice bizarre rites.
      All kinds of egotistic
      Monkey shenanigans,
      Alas, Alas.

21   But whatever the form
      A devotee wishes to worship,
      That faith I strengthen.

22   With faith

Strengthened
He worships
And marvels
At the One.
All his needs are surely provided
As preordained by me.

23   The reward for men
Of ignorance
Is restricted.
Worshipers of the False
End up with their Gods.
My devotees
Come to Me
And see Me
As the One.

24   The ignorant
Think of Me
As having a bodily form
Only.
But I am formless,
They are ignorant
Of my transcendence,
Unchanging, Supreme.

25   Veiled by yogic power
I am not shown to all.
This hypnotized world
Fails to see Me

As the unborn
Deathless One.

26 I know all beings,
Past, present, and future.
None know Me.
I am the All.

27 All beings
Are subject at birth
To delusion
Arising from the psychic
Polarities,
Like and dislike.
And play of the Qualities
And confusion by Consciousness
With their mind-body.

28 Only men of righteous
Harmony
Whose mad folly has ended
Are free from this
Delusion
And love Me as I am,
Firm in their vows.

29 Those who take refuge
In Me
And strive zealously for freedom
From old age and death,

First come to know the Self, Absolute
Consciousness, Awareness,
Peace, Godhead, as the Source
Of their own Being.

30   Those who see me
As linking
The material and spiritual
And all sacrifices
Find Me with their minds
Integrated
Even at death.

VIII

The yoga
of the source

Each chapter of the Gita is a short Upanishad (mystical teaching) in its own right.

Arjuna again questions Krishna.

1   What is Brahman?
    Where is the Self?
    What is Destiny, oh Supreme Spirit?
    What is the reality of this world and
    What is the meaning of heaven?

Here the Gita shifts its emphasis from Prakriti, meaning Nature, to Purashotama, derived from Purusha meaning the spirit in contradiction to Prakriti, Purashotama may be translated as Supreme Spirit. Sri Aurobindo, in his magnificent philosophical commentary on the Gita, stresses the importance of Purashotama as the saving Grace. The Gita sees Krishna here as the personification of the Supreme Spirit, Creative Force, or Divine Will, the Source.

2   What about the meaning
And way of sacrifice?
Also, how do we
Pass through death?

Krishna replied:

3   Brahman is the imperishable Self,
Absolute Consciousness,
Awareness,
Source of all being,
Supreme Spirit,
Godhead,
Spaciousness,
Peace,
Love,
Essential "what-isness."

One's own True Nature is the Self. The force of destiny creates all beings.

4   Perishable Nature
Is the apparent reality
Of this world.
The reality of heaven

Is the cosmic Being,
Or pure spirit.
I am the foundation
Of that sacrifice
In bodily existence.

5   Whoever at death
Remembers me as Cosmic Being,
Supreme Spirit, Brahman,
Absolute Consciousness,
Self Awareness,
Godhead,
Source of Creation,
Returns to Me, undoubtedly.

6   Whatever one thinks of
At death,
There is a grave danger
Of being absorbed in that idea.

7   So at all times remember
Me and fight!
If you have surrendered to Me
As Self, Absolute Consciousness,
Peace, Awareness, Godhead,
To That you will surely come.

8   He who holds his attention
Unflinchingly
To this Yoga of mind training

Breaks in his wild horses
Of the senses, Arjuna,
With vigor and rigor,
Then you shall arrive
To be met and loved by the
Divine, your own Self.

This verse echoes the parable of the Prodigal Son in the New
Testament.

9–10   At the hour of bitter
        Death,
        Which strikes every man and
        Woman
        Sooner or later,
        Center the life force
        Between the eyebrows
        Focus from the pineal gland
        With sheer, laser beam attention,
        Underpinned by love and gratitude.
        Remember, the Source cast your role as
        A seeker
        And not as a mere tread-mill,
        Sensualist wage slave,
        Carrying vast burdens.
        Be grateful,
        Remember Me, thy Sage,
        The ancient,
        The primeval,
        The primordial,

The original,
Your inner ruler,
Sat Guru in your Heart,
Smaller than the smallest
Neutrino,
Greater than the greatest
Galactic system.
Support of the All,
Formless, effulgent,
Shining, brilliant,
Transcending, black darkness;
You shall touch, gracefully,
Easily,
Blithely,
The Supreme
Himself,
Without fail,
This is my promise.

11   I will now tell you of that state which the Vedas
Call "Eternal."
Which passion-free sages
Enter easily,
In quest of which men observe celibacy.

The Eternal is the "Akshara" a state that the ancients believed
could be reached by observing celibacy (Brahmacharya).
This is not obligatory for the householder. The true
Brahmacharya, according to Ramana Maharshi, is one who
abides in Brahman, ie in the Heart.

12–13   At your death
          Shut all the gates
          Of the senses
          Firmly.
          Place the attention in the Heart,
          And retain the life breath,
          Remembering Me
          As Absolute Consciousness,
          Self, Peace, Godhead, Awareness,
          Then chant the divine Aum.
          You shall then reach the Supreme.

14   To he or she who
          Dwells constantly
          On me as Absolute
          Consciousness, Self, Godhead,
          Awareness, Peace,
          I am always there.

15   Having reached me,
          Great ones
          Are not subject
          To the transmigrations
          Of the subtle bodies,
          Which are the mansions
          Of suffering,
          And perishing.
          They have reached
          The Supreme.

16   From the heavens
     Downwards
     All worlds involve
     Transmigration.
     But on reaching me
     As Self, Awareness,
     Consciousness, Peace,
     Godhead, Awareness, Source
     Of your Being.
     There is no return.

17   Those that understand
     The day of universal
     Creation
     And dissolution
     Know that a thousand ages
     Make up one bright day of Brahman
     And a thousand ages
     The dark night.

18   At the scarlet dawn
     Of that day
     All things now issue
     From the unmanifest.
     At the evening
     Of the black night
     They sink back
     Into the same unmanifest.

19   After many births

The same myriads of beings
Merge helplessly
At twilight
And return
At the new red dawn,
After the morning star
Shining in the sapphire sky
Like a diamond,
Awakens mankind from their deep sleep.

20   Beyond this unmanifest
Is another
The Eternal unmanifest
Which never dies.

21   The Supreme State
Is the undying unmanifest
Nothing,
No-thing,
This my highest mansion,
As Absolute
Consciousness, Awareness,
Self, Godhead, Peace, Source
Of all beings,
For those who come here
There is no return,
I assure you.

22   The Supreme
In whom all live

And who permeates all
Can also be reached
By intense devotion.

23   Now, I shall tell you
     When Yogis depart
     Return again.
     And when they never
     Come back.

24   Knowers of Absolute Consciousness,
     Awareness, Godhead, Self, Source,
     Peace, die
     During the bright waxing phase
     Of the moon's silver beams,
     And the rising course
     Of the sun's golden rays
     From winter to summer
     They do not return.

This is a mysterious verse and implies an ancient knowledge
regarding lunar and solar energy which modern man has
lost.

25   Those who die in the
     Dull waning fortnight,
     And when the sun is
     Declining
     From summer to winter
     Return again.

These verses are concessions to the belief in reincarnation, which maintained the Dharma of the population (apara vidya). The advanced view of Ramana Maharshi stated: "There is no reincarnation, it is a product of thought." When the conceptual part of thought is no longer active (through Grace) ie no mind, there can be no idea of reincarnation. No one is born, no one dies, no one is reincarnated. This is the Truth. The body is in Consciousness, an object created by Consciousness to be witnessed as he plays his or her part in the universal (Lila) or drama of life.

26   These two paths,
    The light and dark,
    Are Eternal;
    By one a man exits
    Never to return,
    By another he exits
    And returns.

27   The Yogi who understands
    These two paths
    Is never deluded,
    So Arjuna, remain firm
    In Yoga.

28   The Yogi who knows
    Transcends
    The reward of good deeds
    Coming from scriptural knowledge,
    Sacrifice, austerity, and
    Charity,

He reaches the Supreme
Primal home.

IX

Sovereign knowledge
and mystery

1   To those uncontaminated
    By the detoxified sea-green tinge of
    Envy,
    I shall now reveal
    The Great Secret of Knowledge
    Which when wedded to wisdom,
    Will free you from the folly
    Of harmful action,
    To others
    And yourself.

2   This is the Sovereign Secret,
    The Crowning Mystery,

Sacred.
To be directly experienced
In line with harmonious righteousness,
Easy to perform,
Undying.

Ramesh Balsekar writes that the Sovereign Secret is "Advaita Vedanta," in his commentary on this verse.[1]

3 Those who lack faith
   In the way of righteous
   Harmony
   Never find me
   But return to the mortal
   Treadmill of wage earning slavery,
   Suffering and delusion.

The Gita warns souls to be on the side of the "angels," not the "devils"; it discusses this in Chapter XVI.

4 By Me as my Self
   The whole universe is pervaded,
   All beings are in Me,
   But I cannot be contained
   In them.

The power of the Unmanifest silence pervades "All" and upholds "All" but cannot be contained in it. This is a Vedantic

---

[1] *The Bhagavad Gita, A Selection*, Zen, Mumbai.

paradox, like a Zen koan to baffle the intellect so it gives up and allows intuitive understanding to arise. The Higher cannot be contained in the Lower but pervades the Lower.

5   Although beings exist
In My Nature as Self
They do not exist in
My Supreme Spirit.
See My divine power,
Myself,
Creating and upholding All
But remaining aloof.

6   Just as a hurricane
Which blows everywhere
Lives in space,
So do all beings
Live in me.

Wind moves in space or ether but does not affect it.

7   All beings return
To My Nature
At the end of a cycle,
At the start of the next
I create more bodies once again.

8   Resourcing from my own Nature
I recreate again and again
All beings
Utterly helpless in this power.

Man refuses to acknowledge that he is powerless. All his so-called "doing" is controlled by the combined necessity of innumerable circumstances. In fact, to the surrendered being who has lost his "egotism" none of his actions are his. All acts are from the Source – so the problem of action is then solved in the para vidya or advanced teaching of Advaita Vedanta.

9   Nor do these acts
    Bind me
    I remain unattached
    Like one that has no cares.

10   Under my intense gaze
    My Nature creates all
    Moving and still.
    Thus the universal wheel of life
    Inevitably turns.

11   The foolish ignore me
    Deluded by my human
    Form
    Not realizing my Real
    State
    As Lord of All Beings.

12   With vain hopes,
    Vain actions,
    Vain knowledge,
    The egotistic nature
    Is akin to ogres and demons.

13 But great souls,
Those whose Nature
Has felt the hand
Of Grace,
Worship me as
Absolute Consciousness,
Self, Awareness, Peace,
Godhead.
Single-mindedly
As the undying Source
Of All to their fellow creatures.

14 Ever glorify me
As Self, Absolute,
Consciousness, Awareness,
Peace, Godhead
Firm in dedication,
With undying devotion,
Steadfast, unwavering.

15 Others, knowledgeable
On their way of sacrifice,
Worship me
As the One,
The Other,
The Omnipresent,
The Source,
Consciousness,
Self,
God,

Peace,
Awareness.

16   I am the Vedic ritual,
     The ancient sacrifice,
     The ancestral offering,
     The sweet balsam
     Of healing herbs,
     The magic power
     Of the sacred Mantra,
     The precious, free flowing
     Gayatri.[2]

     Gayatri Mantra
     We meditate on the spirit,
     The Supreme Light
     Of the three worlds,
     Which is above all
     And merits our worship.
     Remover of all illusions
     And ignorance
     May it enlighten our
     Understanding.

17   The precious, free flowing
     Ghee,
     The temple fare,

---

[2] The Gayatri Mantra is regarded as the most potent of all in Hinduism, from the Rig Veda.

The prayers of thanksgiving.
I am the
Father,
The Guardian,
The Mother, ·
The Provider,
The Original Ancestor,
I am all That
To be understood.
I purify
Through the chanting
of Aum.
I am the wisdom
Of the Rig Veda,
The Sama Veda,
The Yajur Veda.

18   I am the sharp Arrow,
The Bow, the skilled Archer,
The Quiver,
And the target.
The Support,
The Aim,
The Upholder,
The Maintainer,
The Lord,
The Godhead,
The Inner Ruler,
The Witness,
The Single Eye,

The Space for happenings
To happen in,
The Home,
The Dwelling Place,
The Refuge,
The Immortal Friend,
The Firm Companion,
The Origin,
The Primal,
The Dissolution,
The Destruction,
The Foundation,
The Corner stone,
The Treasure,
The Victory,
The Imperishable Seed.
Jai!

Divine attributes are now listed showing the paradox of opposites.

19   I bestow burning heat,
      Withhold torrential rain,
      Make arid droughts,
      Make fierce storms,
      Cause devastating floods,
      Make wars,
      Make peace.
      I am both
      Eternal life

And final death,
Being and non-being.

20   The knowers of the Veda
Enjoying the sweet juice of Soma,
The plant of ecstasy
And divine intoxication,
Are purified.
They worship me with
Sacrifice
And reach to heaven,
Where they enjoy the world
Of the Lord of the Gods,
The celestial delights,
In clairvoyant visions.

This is a concessionary verse (apara vidya), along with the next, to traditional religious beliefs. Ramana Maharshi speaking from an advanced standpoint of Advaita said that heaven and other worlds were only a product of thought and as real as the people who believed in them. This world is also a representation of the senses interpreted by thought, Maya. The Lord of the Gods is Indra. Visions are mental projections as a consequence of intense meditation. They take the form of the religious tradition of the visionary.

21   Having enjoyed heaven,
Their desires still active,
They return to mortality
After their merit is spent.

22 To all those who dwell
In Me
Single-mindedly,
I guarantee fulfillment
Of needs and security.

23 Even those who follow
Other Gods,
Who adore them with faith,
Also adore me
Though not correctly.

24 I am, Alone,
Enjoyer,
Master
Of all sacrifices,
Unless they know
Who I am
They fail.

Krishna can be seen as the essential "I am ness" imminent in each heart. Arjuna represents the confused empiric egotistic mind. Asking "who am I?" Ramana Maharshi's way of Self-inquiry brings one back to the Self. One can read the Gita as if one was Krishna. Most people read it as if they were Arjuna.

25 Worshipers of Gods
Go to the Gods,
Ancestors to

Ancestors,
Spirits to spirits.
My worshipers come
To Me
As Self, Consciousness,
Awareness, Peace, Godhead, Love.

26   Whoever gives me
Even a fresh green leaf,
A beautiful flower,
A delicious fruit,
Or clear, crystal water
With love,
That I accept
As it is offered devotedly
By the pure in heart.

The Gita now stresses the religion of love and devotion,
Bhakti.

27   Whatever acts happen,
Eating,
Offering
Austerities
Do them as for Me.

28   Then you shall be
Released
From the bondage of
Your fate
With its beneficial

And malign
Effects.
With attention centered
In the Yoga of Renunciation
You shall come, freed,
To Me.

29   I am
The same
In All,
No one is either hated by Me,
Nor esteemed.
For all those who adore Me
Devotedly
Abide in Me,
I am in them.

Difficult and contradictory statements abound in this chapter. It demonstrates the Source's equanimity, "all men are equal in the sight of God" – because every man and every woman is God playing his or her part in the Grand Lila we call life – the play of the senses and body-mind actions forced by destiny. One must affirm this situation wholeheartedly – this is true surrender. Douglas E. Harding says if he had three wishes they would be that things are, as they are, as they are. This is the grand affirmation of Frederick Nietzsche who said if his life occurred exactly the same again he would re-affirm every moment of his in spite of painful suffering. This is true heroism. This Gita as taught for Arjuna is the *Way of the Hero* as Ramakrishna confirmed.

30 Even a wicked person
That adores Me
Wholeheartedly
Must be seen
As if on the way
Of righteous harmony.
He has now correctly
Atoned and is
Resolved.

31 He soon becomes
Right-minded.
No true devotee of mine
Ever dies
Spiritually.

32 If they come to Me
For sole refuge,
Even those of low birth,
Women,
Merchants,
Servants,
Shall reach the Supreme.

33 How much more
For Holy Brahmins,
Royal Sages,
Having entered
This changing,
Suffering world
They come to Me.

34   With mind set on Me
     As Self, Awareness,
     Absolute Consciousness, Godhead, Peace,
     Be my devotee.
     Sacrifice to Me,
     Bow down,
     Surrender to Me,
     Be harmonized in Me
     As the Supreme,
     So you shall come
     To Me alone.

If the egotistic self-will obeys this injunction to totally surrender, Self-Realization is assured. Ramana Maharshi said
total surrender was impossible without Grace, but partial
surrender was possible for all. Partial surrender, in time, leads
to complete surrender.

X

The glory
of the Godhead

This is a very exalted chapter and gives Arjuna a vision of the Divine at the cosmological level granted by the Grace of Lord Krishna in terms of Vedic mythology.

1   Listen Arjuna,
    Hear my supreme words
    Which will give you
    Well-being
    As you love Me so.

2   Neither the hosts of Gods
    Nor all the Great Sages
    Know my true origin
    For I am

In all ways
The Source.

3   He who knows Me
      Is unborn
      Beginningless,
      A Lord of the worlds,
      Is undeluded among men
      Free of impurity.

This echoes the Advaita concept. There is no one to be born, no one to die, Consciousness is all there is, all there is, is Consciousness, the substratum of existence and the power that makes things apparently happen.

4–5   This is Intelligence,
      Knowledge,
      Freedom from illusion,
      Forgiveness,
      Truth,
      Self-restraint,
      Calm as a still lake
      On a summer's day,
      Reflections,
      Blue skies,
      Warm sunshine,
      Snow capped mountain peaks,
      Air refreshed by pine forests.
      There is Happiness,
      Being,

Awe and Courage,
Harmlessness,
Austerity,
Generosity,
Good and ill fame.
All these states
Arise from Me
Alone.

Mental states are the shadow play of the Self, brought about by the changing Gunas or Qualities, the opposites, the metabolism, and the DNA programming.

6   Seven Great Maharishis,
     Four Ancient Manus,
     Are of my nature
     They emanate from Me
     Along with all creatures.

The Seven Maharishis are Brighu, Marichi, Atri, Pulastya, Pulah, Krathu, and Vashista. The Four Manus are Swayambhuva, Swarochisha, Uttama, Raivata.

These are Guardians of the way of Righteous Harmony, and Cosmic Order.

This chapter draws generously on Vedic mythology.

Mythology states metaphysical truths in a poetic-symbolic way. It is a way of portraying ideas difficult to express in ordinary language which is structurally dualistic and concept based.[1]

---

[1] The works of the late Joseph Campbell explore the validity of mythology.

7   He who understands
      My manifestations
      As Absolute Consciousness,
      Source,
      Peace,
      Godhead,
      Self,
      His power
      Is firm in Yoga
      Beyond any doubt.

Marveling at the glories of creation leads to worship and love of the Source. Man's true nature is Love, and by loving the source of his own being he is loving his own Self as Absolute Consciousness. We are built for loving – but the veiling by egotism obscures this natural tendency. Ultimately, the lovers realize they are from the same Source and fuse as one.

8   Knowing Me to be
      The Source of All,
      The wise marvel
      At Me with love
      And understanding.

9   With attention,
      And life breath,
      Turned to Me
      They teach one another
      About Me,
      And reflect on Me
      Constantly.

They are happy, dance, sing, and rejoice wildly.

10 To those firm
     In Devotion
     I grant the understanding
     By which they reach Me.

11 From compassion
     I, dwelling in their hearts,
     Destroy their dark ignorance
     With the bright Sun of
     Knowledge.

The Sat-Guru dwells in the heart, all we have to attempt is
to turn within, by attention, and merge in Him.
     Arjuna having realized Krishna's being then praises Him
effusively.

12 You are the Supreme Brahman,
     I Dwelling,
     Purifier.
     Eternal,
     Divine Spirit,
     Primeval Godhead,
     Unborn,
     All pervading.

13 Every sage
     Has called you
     Sage of Sages,

Narada and Asita,
Devala and Vyasa, too.
Now you describe your Self to Me.

Narada is the author of the beautiful Bhakti-Sutras, showing how devotion, step by step, leads to non-dualism. Vyasa
is the legendary compiler of the Vedas, the Mahabharata,
the Brahma-Sutras, and the Puranas. Asita and Devala were
famed Rishis.

14   I accept all
      You proclaim
      As true, Lord Krishna,
      Neither gods nor demons
      Know your real nature.

This is Krishna as the macro-cosmic. It is difficult to know
the formless Godhead. It is easier for Man to commence by
relating to a God with attributes as Krishna describes. Man
as microcosm does not know his true Self until taught as
Krishna teaches Arjuna.

15   You alone know your Self,
      Through your Self,
      Oh Supreme One,
      Lord of Beings,
      God of Gods,
      King of Universes.

16   Tell me fully
      Of your divine glory

By which you pervade
All worlds while staying
As you are.

17   How can I know you?
By ceaselessly meditating
On you?
In what aspects may
I see you?

18   Tell me in fullest detail
About your power and glory,
I could listen to your
Life giving words
For ever and ever.

19   Krishna replied.
Yes, I shall tell you
The most outstanding
of My Divine Glories.

20   I am
The Self,
Consciousness,
Love,
Source,
Grace,
Peace,
Space,
Godhead.

I dwell in the hearts of all,
I am the beginning,
Middle,
And end
Of all beings.

Ramana Maharshi said this was one of the most important verses in the whole Gita.[2] As before, I have amplified the term Self into several other words to convey its true fullness of sense to Western readers. Shankaracharya said the Self dwelling in the Heart is the prime aspect of God to be meditated upon. The Ramana Gita has a whole chapter devoted to the Science of the Heart. In poetic rhapsodies such as this sublime chapter, the pink water lotus of the East and the deep red rose of the West often symbolize this indwelling of the Divine Presence in Man.

Lord Krishna now composes a long and beautiful poem with many Vedic mythological references.

21   If God is as the radiant sun
      I am Lord Vishnu;
      Of the nebulae,
      I am the blazing sun,
      Of the winds,

---

[2] Yesterday evening, after the chanting of the Vedas, a young European who came four or five days ago, asked Bhagavan a number of questions. Bhagavan, as usual, countered him with the question, "Who are you? Who is asking these questions?" Unable to get any other elucidation, the young man as a last resort asked Bhagavan which verse of the Gita he liked the most, and Bhagavan replied that he liked them all. When the young man still persisted in asking which was the most important verse, Bhagavan told him, Chapter X, Verse 20 which runs: "I am the Self. Oh Gudakesa, seated in the heart of all beings: I am the beginning and the middle and the end of all beings." (Letters)

I am Marichi.
Of the planetary forms,
I am the silvery moon.

The Sun as God is Aditya. He has 12 names, one for each
month. Vishnu is for January coming after the winter sol-
stice. The winds are the Marichi. Great forces of Nature
affecting this planet.

22   Among Vedas
     I am Sama;
     Among Gods,
     Vasava.
     Of faculties,
     The brain,
     In being, I am
     Consciousness.

The Samaveda are the opening musical hymns of the Rig
Veda, and therefore most highly regarded. Vasava is Indra,
King of the Hindu Pantheon.

23   Of the celestials
     I am Shankara
     Of the Yakshas
     And Vakshas,
     Vittesha of the Vasus Pavaka,
     And among mountains
     Great Mount Meru.

The celestials are Rudras whose work is to turn man towards

the Self through suffering. There are 11, one of whom is Shankara. Both Rudra and Shankara are names of Lord Shiva. Yakshas are intermediaries between the good and the Vakshas are infernal demons. Vittesha is a guardian of riches. There are eight Vasus, the five elements, of earth, fire, water, ether, and air, with the sun, moon, and stars. So we have the structure of the universe sustained by Consciousness. Pavaka is another name for Agni, the Vedic Fire who is an intermediary between Man and the Gods.[3] Mount Meru is the mythological mountain, the center and axis of this world of appearance.

24   Among priests know
Me as Brihaspati,
As chief of celestial
Warriors,
Skanda,
Amongst waters
The ocean.

Brihaspati is Priest to the Gods. In Vedic teaching the Priest is the intermediary between one level of being and the next. Brihaspati is personified as the planet Jupiter and the archetypal Guru, the morning star which awakens man from sleep.

Skanda is the youngest son of the Great God Siva and was the hero who is to slay the great demon Taraka, the human egotism.

Ganapati Muni (the Tamil genius, poet, and saint) believed

---

[3] Sri Aurobindo's *Hymns of the Mystic Fire* are inspired translations of the Hymns to Agni and very potent.

Ramana Maharshi to be an incarnation of Skanda who had come to slay the demon Taraka for modern humanity.

25 Of the Great Rishis
    I am Brighu,
    Of chants
    I am the sacred Aum,
    Among sacrifices
    I am the repetition of the Mantra,
    Of immemorables
    I am as the mighty
    Snow capped
    Majestic Himalayas.

26 Of all trees
    I am the Asvattha,
    Of celestial Rishis
    I am Narada,
    Of the Gandharvas
    Chitraratha,
    And of perfect Siddhas
    The Sage Kapila.

The asvattha is a wild fig tree, a relation of the sacred banyan tree.

Chapter 15 discusses this analogy. It is the same as the bodhi-tree under which Buddha was enlightened. Symbolically, if its seed lands in the fork of any other tree it strikes its root into the trunk and swells until it splits the host tree. Then the seed of knowledge falls into the human heart.

Narada was the author of the *Great Bakti Sutras*. The
Ghandhavas are the heavenly musicians. Kapila was the ex-
pounder of the Sankhya philosophy, which is stressed in the
opening Chapter II of the Gita.

27   Of fine steeds
       I am Ucciasravar,
       Archetypal horse,
       Sired from ambrosial nectar,
       And of magnificent
       Elephants
       I am Airavata.
       Amongst men
       I am their King.

The white horse, Ucciasravar, and great elephant, Airavata,
were miraculous animals that emerged from the ocean when
churned by rotating Mount Mandara by the gods and the
demons. Internally, this is an allegory for the churning (sadhana) of man's nature in the quest and the marvels that arise.
Animals are sacred in Hindu mythology. The cow wandering
on the streets of Delhi causes a huge traffic jam. Here we
slaughter hundreds of thousands for economic reasons when
they catch the 'flu, called foot and mouth disease.

28   Of heavenly weapons
       I am the thunderbolt,
       Of cows, Kamadhuk,
       Of ancestors, Kandarpa,
       Of serpents, the wily
       Vasuki.

The Vajra or thunderbolt is Indra's weapon. Kamadhuk is the wish fulfilling cow who emerged from the ocean churning (see commentary on verse 27). Kandarpa is another name for Kama (like Eros) the God of Amorous Love. Vasuki is the Shakti or serpent power, the Kundalini. This was the rope that rotated Mandara to churn up the ocean.

29 Of hooded serpents
I am Ananta,
Of water gods,
Varuna.
Of ancestors,
Ayyama.
Of controllers,
Yama,
Dreaded Lord of Death.

Ananta is the serpent in which the Lord rests so he is Prakriti, the creative power or will of nature. Ananta means endless. He is supposed to have one thousand heads. Varuna represents the heavens and is Lord of the waters. Aryama was the first ancestor to have actually met the dreaded God of Death – Yama.

30 Amongst the Titans
I am Pralada,
Of recorders
I am time,
Of beasts I am the lion, their king.
And of birds, Garuda,
The son of Vinuta.

The Titans were a race of giants (the Greek word is understood generally) who arrogantly defied the gods. Prahlada was a son of a giant king but for love of the Lord endured torture. Garuda has an eagle's body with a man's head and carries Lord Vishnu on his cosmic journeys.

31   Of purifiers
I am the typhoon,
Of warriors,
The mighty Rama,
Of fish,
The fierce alligator
Of rivers,
The bounteous mother
Ganga.

Rama, like Krishna, was an Avatar of Vishnu. His saga is told in the Ramayana where he rescues his queen, Sita, from the demon king Ravanna with the aid of the strong monkey God-king, Hanuman, in Sri Lanka. He also is the recipient of the Yoga-Vashista the ancient and most explicit esoteric scripture of Advaita Vedanta. Krishna builds up a resonant number of Vedic poetic images to give Arjuna a vision of the One.

32   I am the beginning,
Middle,
End
Of all beings.
Among sciences
I am the science,

Of Self-Realization,
In disputations
I am the logic.

33   Of letters
I am the A.
Of compound words
The double meaning.
In infinity
Am I.
The Sustainer
Who looks all ways.

A is the primal letter and the first phase of the primeval sound Aum. A compound containing two words is double, eg Rama and Krishna makes Ramakrishna.

34   I am
Grim Death
Who eats all
Greedily.
I am the prosperity
Of those destined
To prosper.
I am all Goddesses
Presiding
Over fame,
Fortune,
Speech,
Memory,

Intelligence,
Constancy,
Forbearance.

35   Among the musical
Sama Veda hymns
I am the queenly
Brihatsama,
The Great Gayathri
Amongst Mantras,
Of the months
Margashirsha,
Of joyful seasons
Glorious Spring.

Music has a miraculous power to open the heart and to affect the subtle body (feelings).[4] The Sama Veda abounds with musical hymns. The Brihatsaman hymn is regarded highly because of its sublimity. The Gayathri Mantra is sacred because of its acknowledged potency as a Mantra. Its poetic meter is the highest in Sanskrit prosody. The month Margashirsha (December-January) is regarded as being auspicious for births and prayers. Spring is a time of rejoicing when the earth erupts in magnificent splendor.

36   I am the gambling
Instinct
Amongst cheaters.

[4] The only philosopher to expound a tenable *Metaphysics of Music* is Arthur Schopenhauer. See *World as Will and Representation* in Vols I and II, Dover Press.

The luster
Of the illustrious.
I am Victory,
Effort,
Clarity.

Man's conventional idea of morality does not apply here.
Krishna as the Divine Voice transcends good and evil, which
are relative, man made concepts. Gambling was also a cause of
conflict between the Pandavas and the Kurus. The Pandavas
lost to the Kurus in a gambling game which led to far reaching consequences in the Mahabharata – leading to this war.
Possibly Krishna alludes to this event? Consequences eventually follow from gambling as the war demonstrates.

37 Of the Krishnis
    I am Vasudeva.
    Of the Pandavas
    The wealth.
    Of sages
    Vyasa.
    Of Poets
    Ushanas.

The Krishnis are Krishna's own people (historically – he was
their king). One theory is that the Gita is an anthology of
Upanishads collected by him with added poetry. Vasudeva
is his family name. It also means the Aum. Vyasa is the
legendary author of the Mahabharata of which the Gita is a
part. The Vedas are also attributed to him. Ushanas (known
as Sukra) was a great poet, even appreciated by the Asuras
(demons)!

38   Of those who chastise
I am the whiplash.
Of those who seek,
Victory
I am the statesman.
In secret matters
I am the silence.
Amongst knowers
I am the knowledge.

The whiplash of Krishna symbolizes the rigor needed to train the fiendish beasts of sensuality.

39   I am
The seed of generations
In all beings.
Nor can any being,
Moving or still,
Live without Me.

Krishna personifies divine attributes leading to the Advaitic understanding that all is God and God is all, Consciousness is all and all is Consciousness.

40   There is no end
To my manifestation,
In brief this is
My eternal glory.

41   Wherever there is glory,

Pure,
Prosperous,
Powerful,
It springs from a fragment
Of my splendor!

42 Why Arjuna should I reveal this!
It is enough to know
That upholding this Creation
With a piece
Of My Self, Consciousness,
Peace, Awareness
I am That, I am.

XI

The cosmic vision

Another great mythological poem is introduced by Arjuna thanking Krishna for his revelation.

1   By your deep insights
    Into the landscape of Self
    My delusions are dissolving
    Like a rain drop in the ocean,
    Or night mist in the rays of
    Early morning sun.

2   I have heard
    About the birth
    And death
    Of all beings

And your undying Kingship.
As you spoke,
So be it.
I welcome this,
But I yearn to have vision
Of your Divine Form.

4   If you please will help me
     See "That"
     And now show me a vision
     Of your Undying Self-hood.

     Krishna answered graciously
     With his deepest compassion,
     Love and boundless mercy.

5   Behold my God-like forms,
     Hundred and thousands, innumerable,
     There are
     Many shapes, kinds, colors, and forms,
     Beyond any imagination,
     A network of precious jewels.

Ramesh Balsekar had a similar vision which he described as "The Universe is uncaused like a net of jewels in which each is only the reflection of all the others in a fantastic interrelated harmony without end."

6   Look at the Twelve Adityas,
     Eight Vasus,
     Eleven Rudras,

Two Aswins,
And Seven Maruts.

These are Natural Forces expressed as Divine Beings in the Vedas, all aspects of the One, as is all and everything. Rudras are celestials who turn man Godward through suffering. The Vasus are the five elements along with the sun, moon, and stars. The Maruts are the forces of wind and storm. The Aswins are the Lords of Light, the horsemen who carry us on the path to the Divine.

7   Listen,
    The whole Universe,
    Moving and still,
    Is all centered in
    Me
    As Consciousness,
    Source,
    Godhead,
    Peace,
    Self.
    There is only One Doer,
    Arjuna,
    Understand that!

8   But your eyes will fail if you see my glory,
    So I shall give you divine sight.

9   So Krishna
    Unveiled to Arjuna
    His supreme form.

10   Myriads of openings,
      Mouths,
      Eyes,
      Sights of beauty
      Decked with divine
      Ornamentation
      And weapons of gold wielded on high.

11   Clad in heavenly
      Garlands
      Of tropical flowers,
      Robes, anointed
      With heavenly incense,
      Wonderful,
      Blazing,
      Boundless,
      Facing every way.
      North, West, South, East.

12   If the radiance
      Of a thousand suns
      Were to explode
      At once in the sky
      It would be as my glory.

13   Then in this form
      Of the God of Gods
      Arjuna saw the Whole,
      All the universe,
      How it was
      Fragmented into the many.

14 Arjuna
Was
Astounded,
Coruscated,
Hair standing on end
Harripalated.
He bowed his head,
Crossed his palms
Across his breast
And spoke:

15 Oh, Lord
I see all Gods
In your form
As well as all beings
And Brahman
Resting on his couch
With all the sages
And celestial wise serpents.

16 I see
Your infinite form
On every side.
Numerous limbs
Openings and eyes
Oh Lord,
Of Cosmic Form
There is no end
Middle
Beginning

To you,
I swear.

This vision is echoed in the Purusha Sutra of the Rig Veda.

17 I see you
Wearing your glorious, shining diamond,
Diadem of stars,
Holding your gold imperishable disc and mace,
Shining resplendent everywhere,
Dazzling beyond words and wildest imagination.
Bright as the blazing fire,
Burning as the mid-day sun
In the height of Summer.

18 You are the Eternal!
To be known.
The ultimate treasure
Surpassing all
Previous ones,
And any jewels on the planet,
Red rubies, green emeralds, blue sapphires,
Translucent diamonds, mauve amethysts, yellow
  topazes,
And shining, orange gold.
You are
The undying
Guardian of the harmonious
Righteous way.
You are the Primordial Spirit!

19　I see you
　　Beginningless,
　　Without middle
　　Or end.
　　Grace itself,
　　Infinite in power,
　　Countless limbs.
　　Sun and moon
　　Are your eyes
　　Your mouth is aflame,
　　Your tongue licks fire
　　Scorching the whole universe
　　With your blazing, burning light.

20　The space
　　Between earth
　　And Heaven
　　And all four quarters
　　Of the universe
　　Is pervaded,
　　Percolated
　　By you.
　　As Absolute Consciousness,
　　You are the substratum
　　Of all things.
　　At the mere sight
　　Of your wondrous
　　Terrifying
　　Forms
　　All worlds

Quiver,
Prostrate,
Shake,
Bow,
Tremble,
Surrender,
My eyes are filled by tears.

Tears are signs of purification through Grace and should be honored. Laughter is also purification – an explosion when opposites meet without any buffering. When there is laughter there is "no mind." Laughter and a cup of tea are the hallmarks of Zen.

21   See, the galactic systems
       Of the Supreme Being
       Enter into you.
       Friends of the Maharishis
       And great Siddhas,
       Some in awe
       With folded palms.
       All cry out, Hail! Hail!
       They sing your praises
       With Vedic hymns,
       Ascending to the heights.

22   The Rudras,
       Adityas,
       Sadhyas,
       Viswedevas,

The two Aswins,
The Maruts,
The Ancestors,
The Gandharvas,
Yakshas,
Asuras,
Siddhas,
All gaze
Absolutely dumbfounded
And astounded,
By you.

The hosts of Vedic forces and Deities all combine in this verse.

The Rudras are the "wild ones" often forces of destruction before tamed by Grace. Rudra in the Vedas is the antecedent of Lord Shiva. The Adityas are the Sun Gods of the highest heavens. Sadhyas are the possibility of attaining visions of these deities. The Viswedevas are the Guardians and include sacrifice, intelligence, purpose, desire, determination, dexterity, wealth, truth, love, sound, art, hunger, solidity, and the mysterious link between God and Man. The two Aswins are divine physicians, authors of the Ayurveda. The Maruts are the forces of movement, winds, gravity and magnetism, electricity, atomic power, and so on. The Ancestors are the originals from which we all descend. The Gandharvas are the beautiful choristers in Indra's heaven who chant and sing. The Yakshas and Asuras are diabolical demons (the black spots in the white spots). The Siddhas are those with magic powers. These may be seen microcosmically as aspects of man's subtle body as well as macrocosmically as aspects of the Divine Being.

23   Mighty armed one,
      Seeing your vast form
      With myriad
      Faces, eyes, limbs, bellies,
      Bearing awesome tusks,
      The worlds are appalled
      And shake with terror.
      So do I at your basalt form,
      Encased in emeralds.

We are now shown the dread side of the Cosmic Powers.

24   Seeing you touch the
      Heights of heaven,
      Blazing, red, blue, yellow,
      Green, purple, gold, orange, black,
      Mauve, and white,
      Orifices opened widely,
      Eyes of fire,
      I am terribly afraid
      And fail in courage
      Like a mortal
      In fear of some attack.

25   Seeing your hungry jaws
      And tusks like angry red volcanoes
      In full eruption,
      Portending cosmic doom and dissolution,
      I find no place in my space
      For peace.

Be merciful, I pray, Oh God of Gods,
Safe haven of the world.

Arjuna now refers to the coming battle. The two armies
are still frozen in awe by Krishna's power as he educates
Arjuna.

26–27 All these sons
Of blind Dhritarashtra
Kings of earth
With mighty Bhisma,
Cunning Drona,
Devious Sutabittra,
And my chief, you, Krishna,
Are about to rush
Pell-mell, like wild tuskers
In heat and elephantine rut
Rushing pell-mell into your open
Jaws,
Too fearsome to look at,
Some to be chewed by your sharp teeth,
Their heads to be crushed
To dust,
Like victims of an
Atomic explosion.

28 As the fast flowing torrents
Of great rivers
Such as the Ganges and Saraswati
Rush to the mighty oceans,

So do these epic heroes
Run blindly into your gaping jaws.

29   As evening moths
Fall swiftly to their death
In the candle flame,
So these brave ones
Speed to their death
In your grinning jaws.

30   Devouring all the world
With your fiery appetite,
You lick them up
Like rice on your palm,
While your radiance
Lights up the whole universe
And also burns it
To scorched earth.

31   Tell me
Who you really, really are
With so horrific a form?
I prostrate before you.
I beg, be merciful and
Gracious,
I seek, earnestly, to
Know you.
Oh aboriginal primal
Being.
I am ignorant of your

Real nature.
Why wear a mask?

Lord Krishna answers:

32   I am Time
     For created beings.
     Destroyer of all
     Worlds.
     Even without your
     Skill
     None of these warriors,
     However great,
     Have a cat's chance in hell
     Of survival.

33   So arise! Arjuna
     Wake up!
     Win fame!
     Conquer your foes!
     Enjoy victory.
     By Me alone
     These creatures have
     Already been slain.

34   So slay
     Your dear teacher Drona,
     Your highly revered Bhisma,
     And Jayadratha,
     Wicked Karna,

All other great warriors
I have already slain.
By preordainment,
Be fearless!
Fight!
You shall be victorious
I promise you!

Sanjaya relates the dialogue to the blind king who is listening intently.

35   Hearing these words of
Lord Krishna
Arjuna crossed his palms
Trembling,
Fell before him again,
Kissed his sacred feet,
And said, voice choking,
Shaking with fear.

36   It is but right
Oh Lord Krishna
That the whole world
Is delighted,
Rejoices
In your praise.
Demons fall
Like oaks in a hurricane
To every side,
In incontinent fear.

The hosts of the mighty Siddhas
With all their magic powers
Bow down before you,
Trembling.

37   Why should they not
Prostrate
Before you?
Great one,
Originator even of Brahman,
Boundless God of Gods,
Refuge of worlds,
Thou art Eternal Being,
And eternal non-being,
The "what is" and
"What is not,"
At the same instant
What is more
The Supreme beyond both!

Here we see how Arjuna, under Krishna's influence, has become highly eloquent. He demonstrates the paradox of the opposites as resolved by Advaita philosophy. Things can be true at the relative level, untrue at the metaphysical level, then transcended at the absolute level beyond both.

38   You are the Aboriginal God
The primeval spirit,
The origin,
The Source,
Supreme Universal Refuge.

The Knower
Of all "that is"
And can ever be known.
The supreme haven,
Our whole universe
Is percolated,
Pervaded,
Impregnated,
Substratumated
By you as
Consciousness,
Godhead,
Awareness,
Grace,
Peace,
Source,
Love,
Underlying all forms
Endlessly manifesting in nature
By your omnipotent divine will.

39   You are the wild force
     In the hurricane
     And its still center,
     The black cruel mantle
     Of death.
     The blood-red heat of
     Roaring fire.
     The cool-wet-blue of the
     Boundless ocean.

The soft light of Grace
Reflected by the moon.
Our primeval,
Primordial
Father-mother,
Our first Ancient Ancestor.

This verse covers in order Vayu (wind), Yama (death), Agni
(fire – the Promethean intermediary between Man and the
Gods [the Vicar]). Varuna (the oceans, the moon), Prajapati
(the Ancestor). Gustav Holst transposed important *Hymns
of the Rig Veda* into orchestrated choral works appealing to
Western ears and highlighting these features; they are available on CD.

40   Hail!
Before,
Behind,
On every side.
All is All,
Endless Divine Will,
Immeasurable,
You are all pervading,
Percolating,
Impregnating,
Supporting,
Creating,
And so are That.

41–42   Whatever
I have boldly stated

Regarding you as my friend
But in Reality
Ignorant of your greatness,
For any disrespect
I have shown
At play or at rest,
When eating,
Alone,
Or with others,
I humbly beg your forgiveness,
The Sat-Guru,
In my Heart.

43   You are the Sat-Guru of our world
Bhagavan,
Of the moving and still.
Its wise and revered teacher.
No one will ever be your equal
In all the world.
Who can ever surpass you, Oh Lord
Of infinite strength.

44   So kneeling,
Bowing,
Prostrating my vile body,
Holding onto your lotus feet,
I beg your pardon
Adorable one.
Bear with me
As a fond father

Would with a wayward son,
As a close friend
With a betraying one,
As a true lover
With his failing beloved.

45   I rejoice!
I celebrate!
Now, I have seen
By your Grace
What no man has ever
Seen before.
Yet my body
Is riven with fear and trembling,
Quivering,
Show me now
Only your normal form.
Be gracious, Lord,
The sole haven of all
Suffering worlds.

46   Let me see you, Krishna,
As you were before,
Four armed
As other Gods,
With golden crown,
Mace and disc,
Oh thousand limbed,
Almighty cosmic form.

Krishna replied:

47   Out of Grace
I have shown
My power,
My supreme form,
Splendid,
Universal,
Infinite,
Primeval,
Never seen by anyone else
Ever before,
Never again.

48   I reserve this vision
For you, Arjuna.
Not by another
Will I be seen,
Whether through the Vedas,
Sacrifice,
Study,
Gift,
Ritual,
Or austerity.

49   Never fear,
Never be
Confused!
At having been shown
The horrific side

Of my form.
This, my shadow
As Creator, Maintainer, and Destroyer.
So with fear at an end,
Heart courageous,
See my usual form again.

Ramana Maharshi used to say that visions were mentally in-
duced according to the religious conditioning of the visionary and were therefore from the mind. From Chapter XII
of Maha Yoga by "Who" I quote Ramana Maharshi's own
words on this point.

Vision of the cosmic form of God seen by Arjuna. "Sri Krishna told
Arjuna, 'I am formless, transcending all the worlds.' Yet He
shows Arjuna His 'cosmic form.' Arjuna sees himself, the
gods and all the worlds in it. Krishna also said: 'Neither gods
nor men can see Me.' And yet Arjuna sees His form. Krishna
says 'I am Time'. Has Time any form? Again, if the universe
be really His form, it must be one and unchanging. Why
does He tell Arjuna: 'See in Me whatever you wish to see'?
The answer is that the vision was mental – just according to
the wishes of the seer. Hence it should not be interpreted
literally. It was not a vision according to the Truth of God.
They call it a 'divine vision.' Yet each one paints it according
to its own views. And there is the seer also in the vision! If a
mesmerist shows you something, you call it a trick, but you
call this divine! Why this difference? Krishna gave Arjuna
'divya chakshus' – the divine eye – not 'jnana chakshus'
– the Eye that is Pure Consciousness, which has no visions.
Nothing that is seen is real."

Now we see the giant leap we have to make from the rela-

tive "empiric world" to the real metaphysical understanding
of "what is." Christians will see Jesus; Jews, Elijah; Buddhists,
the Buddha; Moslems, Mohammed; and so on ad infinitum.
Ultimately, "This above all – to thy own Self be true" as the
Bard of Avon wrote in the tragedy of Hamlet. In the end
fear is "ego based." The ego wishes to continue existence.
Death is an awakening from sleep and then a transmigration
who knows where and who cares? As Rumi once said, as an
embryo did you dream of this life. How can you know any
other body you may be born into?

Sanjaya then told the blind king:

50   Having spoken to Arjuna
       Krishna showed his
       Usual bodily form,
       He gently calmed
       Arjuna's fears,
       As the stilling of the breeze
       Makes the blue mountain lake serene.

Arjuna continued to speak.

51   Now I see
       Your usual form
       I am recollected,
       And restored to my own Self.

Krishna replied.

52   It is rare and hard

To see my true form,
Even the Gods long to know That.

53 I cannot be seen
As you have seen Me,
Neither by Vedic study
Nor by austerities,
Gifts, or sacrifices.

54 Only by constant
Devotion, I assure you,
Can I be known
And truly seen
And be entered into.

55 He who performs
Actions for me
Takes me for his refuge
And is devoted to me,
Free from like and dislike
Towards all beings
He comes to me.

XII

Devotion

Arjuna enquired:

1   Of those who meditate
    Upon you
    With form and attributes,
    And those who meditate
    Upon you
    Formlessly, as the undying,
    The unmanifest,
    Absolute Consciousness,
    Which is the better?

2   Those who fix their full attention
    On Me
    As Self,

Consciousness,
Awareness,
Godhead,
Source,
Awareness,
Steadily with great faith
Are the better of the two.

3–4   Those who steadily meditate
On the imperishable,
Indestructible as the diamond gem,
Marvelous as the pole star,
Wonderful as the dawn chorus of birdsong,
Glorious as the desert sunset,
Unmanifest as the consciousness That I am,
Unchanging as the awareness That I am,
Omnipresent, as the Supreme, inside me and out,
Unthinkable, as I am above the mental process,
Indescribable even by a poet,
Stable as the rock of ages,
Immovable as the great Mount Meru,
Eternal as the universe in essence,
Controlling their senses as the charioteer guides
     his steeds
From darting outwards,
Here, there, and everywhere,
Even minded always as a judge,
Working for the welfare
Of his fellow creatures, human, plant, and animal,
They assuredly come to Me.

5   Much harder is the work
    Of those whose minds
    Are set only on the invisible
    Unmanifest.
    The invisible unmanifest
    All alone
    Is not easy to reach.

6–7 But those who whole
     Heartedly
     Surrender all their acts
     To Me,
     Meditate on Me,
     Worship Me
     Single-mindedly
     In the Heart,
     I swiftly save
     From the grim nightmare
     Of the death bound world dream.

The great teaching of Surrender, Ramana Maharshi's second
practice after Self-inquiry is introduced by this verse.

8   Fix your attention
    On Me.
    Singly,
    Center it along with
    Your intellect
    On Me,
    Then you will rest

In Me
Beyond any doubt.

Krishna here represents the Sat-Guru immanent in the
Heart as well as the Transcendent Deity.

9   If you are unable
To reach me this way
Then come by constant
Practice.

10   If this is too hard
Then perform deeds
For my sake,
This will lead to
Perfection.

11   If even this is too hard
Then take refuge in Me,
Senses controlled.
Give up the fruit of actions
And give egoless service
To God, the Source of your Being.

12   Better indeed is knowledge
Than effort based practice.
Meditation is better than
Knowledge.
Giving up the fruit of deeds
Is better than meditation.
From this peace comes.

13–14 He who never hates
Any body,
Is friendly,
Compassionate,
Unattached,
Free of egotism,
Equal in pain and pleasure,
Forbearing,
Content,
Balanced in mind and body,
Controlled,
Firm in faith,
Attention fixed on Me,
Then he, my devotee,
Is dear to Me.

15 He who is unaffected
By the world dream,
Free from the snares
Of excess pleasure,
Anger,
Pain,
Anxiety,
He is also dear to Me.

16 He who has left desires
Is pure,
Prompt,
Unconcerned,
Worry free,

Giving up fruit of deeds,
He also is dear to Me.

17   He who neither exults,
Nor hates,
Nor grieves,
Nor lusts,
Has renounced the absurd distinction
Between so called good and evil,
Devoted,
He also is dear to Me.

18–19   He who is equal
With friend or foe,
In honor or disgrace,
In the cold of Arctic waste,
In the heat of baked desert,
In ecstasy of pleasure,
In depth of pain,
Free from attachment,
To whom praise or blame
Are much the same,
Silent,
Happy with whatever comes,
Unattached,
Steady minded,
Full of devotion,
He is also dear to Me.

20   They who follow

This immortal way
Of righteous harmony
By devotion,
To whom I am Supreme,
Their goal,
Are very, very
Dear to me.

XIII

Knowledge
of the field

1 The Body is the Field,
   He who is fully aware of it
   Is named by the wise
   A Knower of the Field.

2 Know that I am
   The Knower of the Field,
   In all the Fields.
   The knowledge of the Field
   And the Knower of that
   Is true knowledge.

In Ramana Maharshi's selection of the 40 most important
verses in the Gita, he selects this as the second, the first being

II.1, which merely sets the scene.

This verse opens up the way of Self-observation, the impartial witnessing (Purusha) of everything that arises in and from the body-mind organism (the Field). Without this knowledge of the Field a wise, spiritual life cannot take place as we would be at the mercy of every impulse. Witnessing, noticing what arises brings the Field into the light of consciousness-awareness and reduces the identification with the mind-body.

The Purusha (or spirit) is also known as the witness. This chapter discusses the relationship between Purusha (Spirit) and Prakriti (Nature). Self-observation was taught by most of the significant Western spiritual teachers such as J. Krishnamurti, G. Gurdjieff, P. D. Ouspensky and Jean Klein. It is the basic principle behind the Buddhist Vipassana meditation system.

3   I shall teach you
      What the Field is.
      Its Nature,
      Modes,
      Source.
      Who the Knower is
      And what is his power.

4   It is chanted in the Vedas
      And is told in the Brahma-Sutras.

5–6   The Field
      Is broad and made from
      Earth, air, water, fire, ether,

And Egotism.
Its identification with the Field,
And its Reason,
The tool of ego,
The sense organs,
The bundle of thoughts,
Or mind,
The objects of senses,
Desire,
Dislike,
Happiness,
Misery,
The gross animal body,
Intelligence,
Strength,
These make up the Field
And its modes.

This verse is the basis of the Gita's psychological understanding combined with the swing of the opposites and the
play of the Gunas or Qualities.

7–11   Now I shall tell you
What is called Wisdom.
What is not this, is Ignorance.
Humility,
Absence of hypocrisy,
Non-violence,
Forgiveness,
Straightforwardness,

Egoless service to the teaching,
Purity,
Strength,
Control,
Detachment,
Absence of selfishness,
Perception and compassion for the miseries of
    birth,
Death,
Senility,
Sickness.
Non attachment
To children,
Wife or husband,
Home.
Constant equanimity
In so called good and bad
Happenings.
Unflinching devotion,
Solitude.
Distaste for company of ignorant ones,
Love of knowledge of the Self,
Love of philosophical truth.

12   This must be known,
Knowing which one reaches
Deathlessness.
It is the beginningless
Supreme Brahman,
Which is neither being

Nor non-being,
But beyond both.

Again, the Gita points beyond the dualities of the opposites,
the Sat and Asat, Being and Non-being.

13   Brahman has limbs and senses
     On all sides,
     Eyes, faces, heads, ears,
     Arms, legs,
     Everywhere.
     He lives in the universe
     Enveloping all.

Again, Brahman, the formless source of all is personified an-
thropomorphically as a concession to human understanding,
which takes time to perceive the formless metaphysical principle sometimes called in Western philosophy "The Thing in
Itself"[1] (Kant and Schopenhauer).

14   Though he seems
     To be identified,
     Glued to the senses,
     He is free of them all,
     Unattached,
     Supportive of all,
     Free of qualities,
     He enjoys
     Life as it comes,
     Whatsoever.

[1] Paradoxically, the "Thing in Itself" is "No Thing".

15 He is within
And without
All beings,
Moving and still.
He is unknowable,
Subtle,
Far, yet near.

Words fail to describe the indescribable, one can only point out by paradox. The intellect cannot grasp the infinite Brahman. If it gives up, defeated by paradox, intuitive understanding may happen. This is akin to the Zen Buddhist koan, which has the same intention.

16 Undivided,
He seems to be divided.
He supports,
Pervades,
Rules,
Eats,
Generates
All beings.

17 He is the light
Of all lights
Beyond darkness,
He is wisdom,
The bow,
The arrow,
The target,

The aim,
Dwelling in all hearts.

18   So the Field,
Wisdom and its goal
Have been taught
To my devotee,
Who understands
And reaches my place.

This closes the first section on the Field and the Gita now
discusses Prakriti (matter) and Purusha (spirit).

19   Know that Matter
And Spirit
Are without beginning or end,
All Modes
And Qualities
Descend from matter.

20   Matter is the cause
Of the effect,
Of the body
And its senses.
Spirit causes
The experience
Of pleasure
And pain.

21   Spirit lives in Matter,
Enjoys all Qualities

Born from Matter.
Attachment to Qualities
Causes birth
In auspicious or inauspicious
Matrixes.

Matter can be understood as that representation of the organ of perception (the brain) which responds to the senses. Spirit is the invisible element which the senses fail to recognize but can be intuitively understood. Consciousness is Spirit – what appears to the senses in the space of Consciousness is Matter. Matter is subject to time, cause and effect, duration, and can be measured, seen, felt, smelled, heard, and so on. Spirit is not subject to these conditions. In Western philosophy, Spirit is the Noumenon and Matter the Phenomenon. Terms employed by Kant, Schopenhauer, and Balsekar.

22   The Supreme Spirit
Living in the body
Is the witnessing
Consciousness,
The inner-ruler,
Sustainer,
Enjoyer,
Supreme Lord,
Highest Self.

23   One who knows
To distinguish
Spirit
From Matter
With the Qualities

Is not reborn
Although acting
Many roles in life.

24   Some reach the Self,
The Absolute Consciousness,
Awareness,
Godhead,
Peace,
"What Is"
By meditation,
Separating things seen
From the Seer,
Some by philosophy,
Some by the Yoga of egoless deeds.

Douglas Harding, the celebrated contemporary seer, author of many books and now aged 93, helps seekers to separate Consciousness from what is observed. He uses visual aids, masks, mirrors, tubes, amongst other items, for his experiments. In this way many experience an intense recognition of their Consciousness and are thus able to remove the identification with objects that appear in it.

25   Some come to this
Realization
By resonating with teachers
Who know
And so become devoted.
These too, intent on
Listening with attention,

Also cross the ocean
Of spiritual death.
So if one is defeated by
Effort
And Self-inquiry
Surrender,
And so touch
The highest state.

This was Ramana Maharshi's solution to the so called "problem" of Self-Realization, to surrender if the devotee found Self-inquiry too difficult. Most Western teachers advocate surrender. Very few seekers are prepared for Self-inquiry, which requires a focused attention.

The Gita now returns to discussing the Field and its Knower.

26   Know Arjuna
That whatever is born,
Moving or still,
Is born from the union
Of the Field, the mind-body
And its Knower, awareness.

27   He who sees the Supreme
Being
Equally in all bodies,
The eternal amongst the
Perishing
Truly sees.

28 He who sees
    Inquires who is the seer?
    Living "equally" everywhere
    He does not risk
    Destroying the Self
    By the folly of egotism
    And so touches the highest state.

29 He who truly sees
    That all his so-called
    Deeds
    Are carried out by Nature alone
    And that his Self
    Is only the witness,
    Truly sees.

30 When he truly knows
    The "so called" separate
    Existence of being
    Is planted,
    Rooted,
    Watered,
    Pruned,
    Gardened,
    Budded,
    Flowered,
    Fruited,
    And dead-headed,
    In and by the One,
    He trusts That,
    And reaches Brahman.

Robert Adams said trust "what is." To use the gardening analogy – orange trees do not worry about how to grow oranges.

31   The undying
Supreme Self
Of Consciousness,
Godhead,
Peace,
Awareness,
What-is-ness,
Though living in the body
Never does anything,
Nor is attached to anyone,
As she is without a beginning
And is quality-less.

32   Just as the all
Encompassing ether,
So subtle,
Is never tainted
By anything,
Such is the Self.

33   Just as the blazing
Noonday sun
Lights the whole world,
So the Knower of the Field
Lights the whole Field.

Ramana Maharshi said that the Jnani affects the whole world through his silent dynamic presence, even those who have never even heard of him. Sages like Ramakrishna, Ramana Maharshi, Sri Aurobindo, and J. Krishnamurti have mitigated the planetary ambience and ushered in the New Age movement, a stepping stone for many young seekers. Those who make an effort and break through to Self-Realization affect the collective unconscious of mankind. Thus the best way to help humanity is indirectly through Jnana.

34   Those who clearly see,
       With the third eye of wisdom,
       The subtle distinction
       Between the material Field,
       The mind-body organization,
       And the spiritual Knower of the Field,
       Sheer Consciousness, Awareness,
       And also the way to liberate
       Beings from the bonds of nature,
       The separate "will" or ego,
       Reach Brahman.

XIV

The three qualities

The Gita now moves into Advaitic (non-dual) concepts at a
cosmological and psychological level.

1   Now I shall teach you
    About the Supreme,
    The highest wisdom,
    Realizing which
    Many have reached
    Perfection,
    Their true nature.

2–3 Touching this wisdom,
     Those who are One
     With me, in Spirit,

Are not born at the moment
Of illusory creation,
Nor afflicted at the time
Of imaginary dissolution.
Great Nature is my
Maternal womb.
Into it I spill my seed.
Then all creatures
Are born to being.

4   Of all the myriad forms
Born from manifold wombs
Nature, herself, is the
Mother womb.
I am the Father
Who sheds the seed.

5   Active, passionate deeds,
Passive, dark sloth,
Neutralizing, sheer clarity,
These for us
Are born
From Nature.
They bind
The undying spirit
To the mechanistic
Materialistic body.

Rajas, Tamas, and Sattva are now discussed.

6   Of these, sheer Clarity,
Because of its purity
Is illuminating,
Like the sun
Breaking through to light
A dark place.
Flawless,
It binds the transmigrated spirit,
Bird-like,
Which you are
Through its attachment
To things
Mental and physical.
Even by happiness and knowledge,
Oh blameless free one
It binds.

7   Know the crimson
Active force
To be raging and passionate
Like fire
Born from sexually willed
Desire
And identification
With the mind-body
Organism,
Its deeds and expectation
Of rewards.

8   Know that dark, black shrouded

Passivity,
Which deludes all beings,
Springs from ignorance.
It binds by gross error
And despicable laziness
Combined with over-indulgence.

9   Bright white sheer
     Luminous Clarity
     Lead a man or woman
     To happiness.
     Passionate activity to deeds
     And slothful passivity
     Veils wisdom and understanding,
     Urging him or her to error
     And leads to dark suffering.

The words of Jesus, "Take up your bed and walk," and "Gird up your loins" are echoed here. Bringing Rajas to it, the disease of Tamas can be cured and Sattva may result.

10   Sheer blissful Clarity
      Wins,
      Defeating
      Passion and weakness.
      Passion can beat
      Clarity and passivity,
      So beware,
      Worst of all
      Is lazy slothfulness, it can destroy
      Clarity and passionate action.

11   When in the body
With all its sensual gates
Wide open
The light of wisdom comes.
One knows that sheer
Clarity
Has prevailed.

12–13   Miserly and acquisitive
Gluttonous greed
With egotistic motives,
Continued restlessness,
Compounded by insatiable
Desires,
Come from indulging
Overmuch
In passionate action.
When dark, sleeping,
Lazy, slothful passivity
Dominates,
There results
Banal boredom,
Pathetic lethargy,
Blackest depression,
Mad mistakes,
Total delusion.
These devils romp
Playfully
In such a weak mind.

14–15   When one dies
        And Spirit
        Abandons the temporary
        Body,
        If passionate activity
        Is dominant
        His subtle body will be re-born
        Again with those still
        Attached
        To such folly.
        If lazy sloth prevails
        His subtle body will be re-born
        In the womb
        Of ignorant ones
        Or worse still,
        Woe betide,
        Among animals.

16   The adorable gracious
        Fruit
        Of Clarity
        Is clear as the gooseberry
        In the palm of your hand.
        The red-pepper fruit
        Of passionate action
        Ends in despair and sorrow.
        The poison-ivy fruit
        Of black idiocy in eventual insanity
        Or suicide
        Come from lazy, slothful,
        Bed-ridden inertia.

Many mistaken people who come in touch with Advaitic (non-dual) teaching think because they are "powerless" and "can do nothing" they should drop out of life and then have a Tamastic existence. They are even supported by the state under the guise of financial benefits because of psychological problems. This is a gross error. Only a full integration with life, affirming your destined path, following the vocation you are most attracted towards, brings an approximation to happiness. From this change, Grace can operate. As Jesus said: "take up thy bed and walk!"

17   Wisdom springs
      From sheer Clarity.
      Greed thrives on
      Passionate action.
      From laziness arises
      Error, delusion, and
      Ignorance.

18   Those who rest in Clarity
      Climb.
      Those of passionate activity
      Stick in the middle.
      Those of dark, lazy inertia
      Descend.

19   When the seer
      Sees with Clarity
      That he is not the Doer,
      Apart from the
      Interplay of Qualities,

And knows that I am
Beyond them,
He reaches being.
This is discrimination
Which is the first step to wisdom.

20   An incarnated being
Transcending the three qualities
Arising from his or her body
Becomes free
From painful birth,
Agonizing death,
Senility,
Sorrow,
And reaches eternal
Life.

Arjuna asked:

21   What are the marks of the One
Who has overcome the
Three Qualities?
How does he act?
How does he transcend them?

Krishna replied:

22   When either light
Activity,
Or ignorance

Enter
He is not hostile,
Nor resistant,
Nor is he desiring
Them either
If they fail to come.

One welcomes whatever happens as a gift from the Source.

23   As an impartial witness
He is not disturbed
By the play of the three Qualities.
He stays firm,
Unwavering
As action proceeds from them
In due course.

24   He is the same
In excruciating pain
Or ecstatic pleasure,
Self-assured.
A brown clod of mother earth,
A dense stone of mountain rock,
A glistening nugget of shining gold,
The enjoyable,
And the disliked.
Praise or blame.
He sees all as equal.

25   The same

In fame
And disgrace,
With good friends
And hostile foes.
He who surrenders
The lead
In joint undertakings
Is called
One
Beyond doubt.

26   He who serves Me
With love
Undeviating
Totally transcends
The Qualities
And merges
In Brahman.

27   For I am the home of Brahman
That is eternal,
Imperishable,
Perennial,
Blissful.

XV

The supreme being

This is a beautiful, mystical, lyrical poem inserted into the Gita, introducing the Supreme Being (Purushottama). Aurobindo gives great emphasis to this saving Grace of the Gita in his Commentary. He wrote that with this doctrine, the Gita is all that is necessary for the spiritual life.

1   The Pippal Tree, the Banyan Tree
Which hangs its boughs below,
Its roots above,
Is an eternal symbol.
The leaves are the sacred hymns
Of the Vedas.
He who knows this, understands
The Vedas.

2   Its branches silver, splay above, below,
     Growing well on the eager play of the Qualities.
     The objects of sense leap to kiss the sun and air
     And are its flowering.
     Its hanging roots reach below the
     World of Man,
     Tending to binding deeds.

3–4   A tree's reality
      Cannot be understood
      By sight alone.
      It is an energy in process.
      After cleaving this deep
      Rooted tree
      With the strong axe of
      Non-attachment,
      And discrimination,
      That state should be found
      From which on reaching
      One never returns
      To the world of illusion,
      Saying, "I surrender
      To the Supreme Spirit
      From which this ancient
      Pulsation of creation
      Starts to flow."

Apart from the Source (Brahman) the world does not really
exist. It is an appearance in Brahman (Consciousness). A
sensual representation interpreted by the brain and so a

creation of the mind (Maya). To quieten the mind and turn it towards the Self (inquiry) is the way to reach Brahman. There is always an interplay between the empiric every day and metaphysical world in this poem. This paradox has to be entertained. We live in two worlds, with humor we enjoy the relative and do not bore others by lecturing from the standpoint of the Absolute. A trap many earnest devotees can fall into.

5　The de-hypnotized,
　　Those freed from pride
　　And ignorance
　　Who have conquered
　　Attachment,
　　Devoted to the Self,
　　Turned away from lusts
　　Beyond the opposites
　　Of excruciating pain
　　Or orgasmic pleasure
　　Reach that undying state.

6　Neither sun in full blaze,
　　Moon in coolest Grace,
　　Nor flaming fire,
　　Illumine this state,
　　From which on reaching
　　One never returns.
　　This is my supreme home.

7　A fragment
　　Of my Self

Eternal
Becomes
Individuated
As a separate soul
In this world dream
And wins to itself
The six senses
And the intellect
Based on Nature.

8   When God Almighty
Assumes a body
And when he departs
He takes the six senses
And leaves like the wind
That wafts the scent
Of roses.

This would apply to great souls like the founder of world
religions and in modern times sages like Ramakrishna
Parahamsa, Vivekananda, and Ramana Maharshi.

9   Ruling
Over sensitive ear
With magical eye,
Tender skin,
Eloquent tongue,
Refined nostril
To all odors
Sweet or foul,

And the precision
Of intellect,
To enjoy the
Games of this world-play
As long as I am in the body.

10　　The poor ignorant
Deluded fool
Never sees Him
As the indwelling Self.
Whether with the three Qualities,
He leaves the vile body,
Or enjoys psychic experiences,
Only those who have
Opened
The third eye of wisdom
Truly see clearly.

11　　With strenuous concentration
Yogis
Find Him dwelling within
But ignorant ones
Even if they strive like
Bullocks
Fail to see Him.

12　　The radiance of the sun
Which illumines
The whole world,
And that which is in the moon,

In fire,
And in the heart,
Know that to be My
Lustrous glory.

13   Entering
      Dear Mother Earth
      I sustain
      All beings and creatures
      With my powers.
      As the sacred Soma,
      The strength-giving liquor,
      Like the silver moon
      I feed all plants and creatures
      Till refreshing morning dew descends.

14   Having entered the earth
      As volcanic fire
      And into the bodies
      Of men and women
      As Divine spirit
      And joining
      With the life breath
      And life-force
      Moving up and down
      I eat and enjoy
      The nourishment inherent
      In all fresh foods.

15   I live in every Heart.

From Me
Issues memory and knowledge
As well as their loss.
I am He
To be known by the Vedas.
I am also the author
Of the sacred Vedas
And its Knower.

16   There are two spirits
     In the world.
     The dying and the undying.
     The dying includes all creatures.
     The undying is unchanging
     For eternity.

17   There is another
     Over and above
     The highest,
     The Supreme Self.
     He is the undying Lord
     Who entering
     Hell, Earth, and Heaven
     Sustains them all.

Hell and heaven may be seen as states of mind.

18   Since I surmount
     The dying
     And am the undying

I am known
In the world
As in the Vedas
As the Supreme.

19   The de-hypnotized
Who knows me
As the Supreme
Are all-knowing
And love Me
With their whole being.

20   I have unveiled to you all
Oh unblemished ones
The Supremest Secret.
One who knows this becomes wise
And reaches the fulfillment of life.

Contradictions and paradoxes abound in the higher teaching to defeat the conceptual intellect. Bruno said: "The walls of heaven are based on paradox." Each brick of contradiction added to the wall, in time, unbalances it and it will collapse leading to Enlightenment. If a statement is not paradoxical it may not be true?

XVI

The God-like and
the devilish

Krishna speaks.

1–3 Arjuna,
        One who is born
        With heroic virtues
        From the divine nature
        Is fearless,
        Pure,
        Set in calm wisdom,
        Charitable,
        Open-hearted to all suffering beings
        Who because of their destiny
        Are in need
        To be benefited by you who are

Affluent.
Self controls your wild horses,
Sacrificing your desiring will
To power.
Wise in studying scriptures of
All religions.
Repentant,
Straight forward,
Non-violent,
Truthful,
Anger-free,
Resigned,
Peaceful,
Benign,
Compassionate,
Lust-less,
Soft,
Tender,
Yielding,
Open-handed,
Gentle,
Discreet,
Equitable,
Brilliant,
Forgiving,
Brave,
Pure,
Hate-free,
Without pride or
Egotism.

4   Those born, alas,
    With tendencies
    Of a devilish nature
    Are marked
    By murky hypocrisy,
    Impish arrogance,
    Pompous pride,
    Puffed up self-conceit,
    Sudden anger,
    Cruel harshness,
    And blind ignorance.

5   It is ordained
    That attributes of divinity
    Lead to liberation
    While those that are devilish
    Lead to bondage.

Once again the Gita is dualistic for sociological reasons. From an Advaitic standpoint good and evil come from the one Source to sustain the melodramatic Lila, or Divine Play. The Gita wishes to point out qualities to be avoided by the populace. These verses are also moral pointers for aspiring seekers. They are polar opposites, and like the Ying and Yang symbol there is a black spot in every white spot and a white spot in every black spot.

6   There are two types,
    Divine,
    Demonic.
    The Divine is well known.

I shall tell you about
The Demonic.

7   Demonic men and women
     Fail to understand
     Performance of right or
     Wrong deeds.
     They are often neurotic
     If not psychopathic,
     There is neither purity,
     Character,
     Or truth in them.

C. G. Jung who studied the Gita would say that this is the
shadow side of men and women, which instead of being
rejected must be accepted, if not approved, whenever it appears. Harmony is resolving the good and evil in ourselves.
In every white spot there is a black spot. Harmony is the
reconciliation of polar opposites.

8   The ignorant say
     The world is baseless,
     There is no God,
     Ill conceived,
     Some cosmic mistake.
     They pour scorn on the sacred.

9   Digesting these views,
     Wretched sufferers
     Of little understanding

Perform reckless deeds
Full of ill-will
That would lead our world
To chaos and often does.

10   These men and women,
      Impure,
      Obsessed by lust,
      Hypocrites,
      Conceited,
      Intoxicated,
      Deceived by materialist
      Philosophy,
      Confused,
      Are intent to perform
      Criminal deeds.

11   Entertaining endless
      Passions,
      Often ending in painful death.
      They think gratification of the senses
      Is the highest good.
      Being cocksure,
      The purpose of life
      Is to revel in sensuality.

One only has to observe the modern cinema (Cinemaya) to
note this comment.

12   Firmly fastened

In bondage,
Tied by a hundred ropes
Without any hopes
They deceive,
Wax wrath,
Plotting to acquire more and more riches
By unjust means,
Fat cats creaming enterprises
And exploiting the public
For sensual pleasure.

13–16 Hypnotized by ignorance
Saying "I have attained this"
And tomorrow
"I shall attain that."
"It will become mine, mine!
This foe, I have destroyed.
I am the Lord,
Enjoyer,
Perfect,
Strong.
Rapturously happy,
Rich,
Wellborn,
Handsome,
Who else is like me?
I shall now give to a charity
And then celebrate
With strong drink."

These idiots
Distracted by glamor and glitter
Fall down! Their subtle bodies
End up in murky swamps.

17   Egotistic,
Stiff necked,
Rich,
Proud,
Intoxicated,
Constipated.
They ape obeisance in church or temple
In lip service only.
Ostentatiously craving
To be honored
By the secular power.
Such obscenity!

18   Fanning themselves
Like peacocks
In egotism,
Believing all their success
Is gained by their own efforts.
Such arrogance!!
They believe in
Force to subjugate
Opponents.
Fawn to be adored
By the mob as celebrities.
Passionate in numerous

Extra-marital affairs.
Heterosexual, homosexual,
Lesbian, sadistic, masochistic.
They identify with their
Own obscene
Bodies
Which they admire in
Mirrors.
They spend vast sums
On vitamins, cosmetics,
Face-lifts and surgery
To support their revolting
Image,
Which they think is beauty,
Hungry for fame;
The angels weep.

19   Into the depths of devilish
Wombs,
I cast cruel savage haters,
Decadent degenerates,
Unholy,
They shall be reborn
For more and more suffering
Until they repent,
Through inevitable remorse.

This chapter is dualistic. Sociologically it wishes to discourage bad behavior in a society that was un-policed. This social conditioning succeeded for thousands of years. It is the "apara vidya" or lower teaching of Shankara.

20 These foolish idiots
Born in inauspicious wombs
Again and again
Reach the fallen condition,
They fail to reach Me.

21 The threefold gates
To hell
Are
Sexual passion,
Wrathful anger,
Monetary greed,
One must give up this
Demonic trio.

Ramakrishna condemned lust and gold as the arch enemies
of spiritual enlightenment.

22 A man or woman
Free from these three,
Works out his own
Synthetic good,
And through Grace,
Reaches the pinnacle.

23 He who abandons
The injunctions of the scriptures
And behaves according to
Willful impulse alone
Attains neither salvation
Nor happiness.

24   Let scripture
      Be your authority
      In deciding what is
      Right and wrong.

This chapter ends in a massive paradox when it tells you
to obey scripture, contradicting its previous statements
condemning those who follow the letter of the law. The
intelligent seeker is enjoined to transcend both these
opposites and be His Self beyond the linguistic, semantic,
opposites, appropriate in one context, inappropriate in
another.

XVII

Faith

Arjuna asked Lord Krishna:

1 What is the Nature,
   Clear, passionate, or dull,
   Of those men and women
   Who renouncing the letter
   Of scripture
   Worship, nevertheless, with faith?

2 Faith
   Is inherent, hidden,
   In all men and women
   But it may be
   Clear, passionate, or dull.

3   Faith
      Of each is according to their Nature,
      In essence all are endowed
      So what their faith is, so indeed
      He or she is.

4   Those blessed with Clarity
      Worship the Source of their
      Own being,
      Those with passion worship
      False gods.
      The dullest worship corpses,
      Ghouls, and spirits.

5–6   Those men and women
      Who practice rigorous
      Austerities
      Not set down in scripture
      Are full of hypocrisy,
      Egotism,
      Desire,
      Passion,
      Needlessly
      Torturing their bodies
      And senses.
      I their inner ruler
      Know them to be demonic.

7   Food, precious to all,
      Has three qualities,

So does sacrifice,
Austerity,
Charity.

8   Delicious fresh vegetable,
Dishes with milk delicacies
Foster a long life,
Vital strength,
Intelligence,
Energy,
Health,
Happiness,
Delight,
Nourishment,
Enjoyment,
And are best for clarity.

9   Bitter dishes,
Sour,
Too salty,
Too hotly spiced,
Too piquant,
Give indigestion.
Animal meats, poultry, and fishes,
Excessive alcohol,
Lead to swelling of the stomach,
Flatulence,
And diseases of the colon, liver, and bladder.
All these foods
Are adored by gluttonous men of passion.

10   Stale grub,
      Insipid,
      Putrid,
      Polluted,
      Rotting,
      Undercooked,
      Overcooked,
      Greasy,
      Junk food,
      Left-overs,
      Are impure
      And slopped by sleepy, lazy ones,
      Who invariably vomit.

11   Sacrifices
      Performed scrupulously
      Out of a sense of duty
      As prescribed
      By the Vedas,
      Never expecting any reward,
      With balanced mind,
      Is Clarity.

To love God with all your heart, all your soul, and all your might, and all your mind, for his own sake alone and not even for the sake of Self-Realization is auspicious. It is then seen to be only the worshiper and the worshiped recognizing that they are identical, the One. The One plays hide-and-seek with his own Self, such is the Lila (divine play) of life, to be affirmed.

12   Know that sacrifice to be passionate,
Ornamented by luscious, delectable plums,
In expectation
Is garlanded with ostentatious pomposity.

13   Sacrifices
Performed
Where pure food
Is not distributed
Equally,
Without the sublime music
Of chanting hymns,
And without payment offered
To the officiants,
Is faithless
And very dull.

14   Worship of the Gods,
True Brahmins,
Wise elderly persons,
The transparent,
The straightforward,
The continent,
The non-violent,
The decent,
These are the true austerities for body-
Mind organisms.

15   Be
Truthful,

Agreeable,
Eloquent.
Use
Poetic,
Auspicious
Language,
Which never annoys
And enjoy scripture-study,
These are the austerities
Of speech.

16   To be
Calm,
Gentle,
Silent,
Controlled,
Pure,
These are the mental
Austerities.

17   These three austerities,
Performed
With faith
And no craving
For fruits of deeds
Are Pure.

18   Any austerity
Performed

For pride,
Honor,
Or to gain
Esteem, for show,
Is unstable and
Passionate,
To be shunned
Like the plague.

19 The austerity
Practiced with
Bodily torment,
Out of delusion,
Or to hurt others
Is black indeed.

20 Any gift
Made freely
With no thought
Of reward,
But as a duty
Given at a proper
Time
To a worthy man
Or woman
Is pure and brightly white.

21 The gift
Made reluctantly
With hope of reward

Is passionate,
And crimson.

22   Gifts made to disreputable
People
In a seedy place
At the wrong hour
With contempt
Are dark and black.

23   Brahman
Is the triple
Aum
Tat
Sat.
By these words
At the origin
Were created
The Brahmana Sutras,
The Vedas,
And orders of sacrifice.

The Commentary on the Brahmana Sutras by Shankara is the classic text of Advaita Vedanta. This, along with his commentary on the Bhagavad Gita, and Ramana Maharshi's *Forty Verses* on Reality are key texts.

Aum is the highest Mantra, the primeval sound. Tat is the transcendental witness of all (Consciousness). Sat is reality and righteousness.

24   Hence any sacrificial

Gift,
Austerity,
Scripturally ordained,
Must start
With the auspicious
Aum chant.

25 By uttering
Tat
The deeds of
Sacrifice,
Austerity,
Gifts,
Are performed by
Seekers of freedom
Without seeking any reward
Whatsoever.

26 Sat means
Reality or
Freedom from illusion,
Righteousness,
And praiseworthy
Deeds.

27 Firmness
In sacrifice
Austerity,
Gifts,
Is also

Sat,
As well as
Deeds for the sake
Of Sat.

28   That which is
Given
In sacrifice,
Charity,
As an austerity,
Or deeds
Done without faith
Are "asat,"
The opposite of Sat.
They are counted
For nought in
All worlds,
Real or imaginary,
I assure you.

XVIII

Freedom and surrender

Eighteen is a sacred number, as it carries digits which add up to nine, as with the Enneagram of the Pythagoreans or the Enneads of Plotinus. Hymns in praise of gods and sages are often of 108 verses.[1]

This last chapter is a highly inspired summation of the whole book.

Arjuna spoke:

1   Krishna,
      Tell me the true meaning
      Of renunciation

---

[1] See Appendix 3 for a fuller explanation.

And abandonment,
Please!

Sannyas is renunciation. Tyaga is abandonment.

2   Renouncing actions
       Prompted by desires
       Is renunciation.
       The giving
       Up of the tempting fruit of all
       Results is abandonment.

3   Some sages say
       Action should
       Be renounced
       As it leads
       To bondage.
       Others say that
       Sacrifices,
       Gifts,
       Austerities,
       Should not be
       Abandoned?
       Please help me.

Krishna replies:

4   Hear from me now
       The triple truth
       About abandonment.

5 Sacrificial
Deeds,
Austerities,
Gifts, should not be
Abandoned.
For wise men and women
They purify.

6 These deeds
Should be performed
Without desire for any reward.
This is my firm and best
Conviction.

7 Renunciation of deeds
Because it is stated by scripture
Is clearly wrong.
Abandonment from
Ignorance
Is an excuse for dark, dense, dullness.

8 He who abandons deeds
As leading to suffering
Out of fear
Fails to receive the benefit
Of abandonment
And is passionate by Nature.

9 That abandonment
Has the quality of Clarity

Which performs deeds
From duty alone,
Renounces attachment,
And desires for hope of any reward.

10   He or she who does not dislike
An unpleasant deed
Nor is attached to
A pleasurable one
Has the quality of Clarity.
He or she has intelligence.
His or her doubts have flown away
Like swallows from the winter frost.
He or she is then
Attuned to harmonious, righteous
Abandonment.

Whenever the Gita uses he it also implies she. But it would be tedious to repeat it every time. In this verse I have demonstrated the double intention.

11   It is utterly impossible
For a mind-body system
To renounce deeds
Totally.
But he who renounces
The rewards for deeds
Is a man of real abandonment.

12   Triple are the rewards

Of deeds.
Evil,
Good,
Or a mixture.
It mounts up after death
To whoever has not "abandoned"
But never to those who "renounce."

The Gita makes a very subtle distinction between renunciation and abandonment. It is as if it is intellectually teasing
us with paradoxes when the words mean almost the same
thing. This intellectual teasing like the Zen koan makes the
mind give up in despair and so opens the way for intuitive
understanding. Perhaps one has to transcend the distinction between abandonment and renunciation. Renouncing
them both as concepts and abandoning even this idea as a
concept.

13–14   Listen to Me for the five forces
That make deeds happen.
This is an important key.
The body,
The imaginary sense of doership,
The brain and sense organs.
The conditioned programmed thought patterns
And ultimately divine providence or
The Will of God or the Source,
Are the authors of all deeds.

There is only one Doer! Ramesh Balsekar stresses that
destruction of the false sense of "doership" is equivalent to

reaching the "ultimate understanding." Thought patterns are an interplay between the DNA and what is cognized from outside, ie conditioned.

15 Whatever deed
Either suggested
Or forbidden
By scripture
Man appears to do,
Either through body,
Speech,
Mind,
Senses,
Is finally, the will of God,
Or the Source.

16 A man or woman
Whose understanding
Is full of perversity
And thinks "I am the Doer."
For dark, dull reasons of conceit
Does not truly perceive the truth.

17 He who is free from egotism,
With a pure mind,
Never really kills anyone,
Nor is he bound by the idea of killing,
Even if he killed everybody in sight.

Egotism is meant to point to the selfishness of narcissism. It includes the wandering perverted conceptual mind but not the functional, working empiric mind necessary for meeting life as it comes. Sages are exact in exercising precise attention in dealing with life as it comes.

18   Knowledge
And its aim
And the Knower
Are the triple
Spurs to action,
While the senses
Are the triple
constituents
Of action.

19   Knowledge,
Deeds,
And the "sense of doership"
Are the triple forces for making things
Happen,
According to the play
Of Qualities.
Now listen.

20   Know that knowledge
To be Clarity
Which sees One Consciousness in all creatures
As essentially the same.
Although differing, there are many modes of
   expression
And behavior.

21 That knowledge
Which sees differences
Among all creatures
Through judgmentalism
Is passionate.

22 That stupidity
Which clings to one aspect of
Creation
As if it was the whole,
Forgetting the One Source,
These are dull, dark, dense
Habits, indeed Arjuna.

23 That deed
Prescribed either by scripture
Or by social necessity
And personal needs,
If performed
Dispassionately
Is deemed to be from Clarity.

24 That deed
Performed egotistically
And with stress
Because one desires fruits of
Approval, applause, reward,
Or riches
Is very passionate.

25 Any deed
    Done from ignorance
    Without taking into account
    The probable consequences,
    Such as loss,
    Violence,
    Incapacity,
    Is said to be
    Dull, dense, and dark.

26 To be an instrument of the divine will,
    Free from any attachments
    And egotism,
    Endowed with firmness,
    Strength, stability, and ability,
    Equal in success or failure,
    Is in "Clarity."

27 That fool who thinks
    "He is the Doer"
    Is passionate,
    Cleaving after a lush fruit salad
    Of deeds,
    Greedy,
    Violent,
    Impure.
    Slave of elation
    And dejection.

28 The fool who thinks

He is "the Doer"
Is lazy,
Crude,
Dull,
Arrogant,
Deceitful,
Wicked,
Weak,
Depressed,
Always postponing action.
He is dark, dense, and deluded.

29   Now listen
To the triple division
Of intellect and stability
According to their modes.

30   That intellect is pure
Which can discern clearly
Between when it is wise to act
And when it is better to refrain.
Between what is wise to try
And what should not be tried.
Between fear and fearlessness,
Bondage and liberation.

31   The intellect is
Passionate
When it fails to
Discriminate

Between the righteous, harmonious
Way
And its opposite.
Between what should be tried
And what should not be tried.

32 The intellect
    Is dull and dark
    When clouded by ignorance.
    Wrong knowledge
    Promotes the opposite
    Of the righteous, harmonious
    Way
    Most perversely.

33 Steadfast stability of mind
    Is Clarity.
    The mind,
    Senses,
    Life breath,
    Are controlled through Yoga.

34 That steadfast stability
    Is passionate
    When held by the fanatically, piously, bigoted,
    And fools who seek riches and lust after endless
    Desires.

35 That steadfast stability
    Is dull and dark

When stupidly
One over indulges,
Is timid,
Despairing and
In spite of it all
Proud.

36 Now listen
To the triple
Happiness,
How to find
Delight,
Ending sorrow.

37 That happiness
Is Clarity
After Meditation
On the Self, as
Consciousness,
Awareness,
Godhead,
Peace,
Space,
Source.
It is as poison at the start
But nectar at the end.

At the beginning, meditation on the Self is difficult and throws up all the impure tendencies repressed and in the unconsciousness. After these are released into the light of awareness, meditation of the Self becomes peaceful and blissful.

38   That happiness
     Is passionate
     Which starts
     As nectar.
     When using objects as aids
     Is poison at the end.

Meditation on an object, a photo, idol, etc can be blissful at the start but poison at the end when the meditator realizes that the Self is the Heart, immanent, and not out there in an object of bodily form.

39   That happiness
     Is dark, dull, and deluded,
     Born of sleep,
     Lazy,
     Negligent,
     Which hypnotizes the
     Mind
     Through believing I am only the body,
     At the beginning, middle,
     And end.

40   There is nothing
     Existent
     In any world
     Free from the triple modes
     Born of Nature.

41 The duties
    Of priests,
    Warriors,
    Merchants,
    And servants
    Are divided
    As to the qualities
    Of their Nature
    And their differing
    Triple modes.

42 Calm,
    Control,
    Restraint,
    Austerity,
    Inside and out
    Purity,
    Forgiveness,
    Honesty,
    Knowledge,
    Wisdom,
    Faith.
    These are the Qualities of the Brahman from
        their Nature.

43 Heroism,
    Courage,
    Resolution,
    Readiness,
    Charity,

Nobility.
These are the duties of
The Warriors,
Natural to them.

44   Farming and
Trade
Are the duties of
The merchant,
Born from their Nature.
Service is the
Duty of the servant,
Natural to his or her
Inclination.

45   Man
Reaches perfection
By engaging
In his own duty.
Listen how he reaches
Success.

46   Man reaches
Perfection
By performing his duty
As worship of the Source
From whom all creatures
Are born.
By whom all is
Pervaded.

This is rare in the West but often noticed in Islamic countries and in country districts of India where Hinduism is still alive.

47   Better is one's own
Duty,
Even if worthless,
Than to attempt
The duty
Of another,
However excellent,
Even if it seems to be worthy.
To perform one's
Own duty
As destined
Is to be free of wrongdoing
And is the divine will of the Source.

48   Never abandon
One's natural duty
Even if defective.
All deeds are somewhat defective
Just as a bonfire
Is enveloped in smoke.

48   A mind
Free from desires,
Controlled,
Unattached,
Reaches

Perfection
In Brahman
By renunciation.

50   Know from Me
Briefly
How a man or woman
Who has reached
Perfection
Realizes Brahman,
The highest
Consummation of
The Yoga of Wisdom.

51–53   One with strong powers of reason,
Controlled,
Steady,
Abandoning sensuality,
Non-attached,
Without dislike
Or excessive liking,
In solitude,
Enjoying study,
Eating a little pure food,
Speaking little,
The body and mind quiet,
Is always in the Yoga
Of Meditation,
Without passions,
Egotism,

Violence,
Pride,
Lust,
Wrath,
Greed,
And the feeling of "mine"
Having been renounced.
He or she is peaceful.
And worthy
To become One
With Brahman.

54   Uniting with Brahman
The calm one
Neither mourns
Nor desires,
Seeing all equally,
He reaches the highest peak
Of devotion.

55   Through devotion
He knows Me
And my Nature
As Consciousness, Space,
Awareness, Peace, Love,
Godhead, Source,
"What-Isness,"
In Truth.
In this Truth,
He unites with Me.

56　And he or she
　　Performing deeds
　　With Me
　　As their refuge,
　　And My support,
　　Through My Grace,
　　Reach the eternal
　　Undying Mansion of Peace.

57　Surrendering
　　All deeds to Me
　　As Consciousness, Source,
　　Godhead, Peace, Love,
　　Space, Awareness,
　　Seeing Me as
　　Representing the Supreme.
　　Then concentrating the mind
　　On my form
　　And formlessly,
　　Fixing their attention
　　On That
　　In one's own Heart,
　　Is bliss.

58　Abiding in Me
　　You shall surely
　　Conquer all
　　Obstacles
　　Through Grace;
　　But failing to hear Me

Through egotism
Is spiritual death.

59   If, Arjuna,
      From egotism
      You decide not to fight
      For the way of righteous
      Harmony,
      This resolve
      Is in vain.
      For, I tell you,
      Really you have no choice.
      Nature will force
      You to fight!

All the moral injunctions of the Gita are pointers, to influence action. What eventually happens is ordained. Strictly speaking choice is only apparent, part of the structure, of predetermination. One has to exercise apparent choice, to the best of one's ability knowing in reality there is no choice. It is part of the Lila. Free will[1] does not stand up to serious philosophic analysis in a world where everything is holistically interconnected. Only after Self-Realization does freedom exist – but until we reach that state its action is speculative. It is inner rather than outer.

60   I assure you,
      Arjuna,

---

[1] For a devastating critique of free will see Schopenhauer's prize essay on the Freedom of the Will.

Even that which you hate
To do
Because it seems deluded,
As you are
Bound by destiny,
Dictated by your Nature,
You shall surely do,
Even against your
So-called will!

Many mystics have confirmed that they are dragged to Self-
Realization by the Divine Force even against their apparent
will.

61 The Lord
    Dwells in the Hearts
    Of all
    Spinning beings,
    Like tops,
    By the triple forces in Nature,
    As if placed
    On a turn-table,
    Around and
    Around.

62 So surrender!
    With all your heart,
    Soul, and might.
    Through Grace you shall
    Surely reach

Supreme Peace
And your Everlasting Home.

63   This wisdom,
     This open secret,
     Of all secrets
     I have given you,
     Reflect,
     And then do whatever
     You like.

We are afraid of freedom. As Ramesh Balsekar points out
over and over again – what are you afraid of? If it's God's
will for something to manifest it *will* and if it is not it *will*
not. So do what you like, it is all in God's hands one way or
another. Only the slave of God is free, as Douglas Harding
once formulated this same truth.

64   Listen once again
     To my Supreme Teaching,
     The most open secret
     Of all secrets.
     I shall tell you what
     Is good for you
     As you are my beloved.

Tony Parsons, the English teacher, has written a very clear
exposition of Advaita called the *Open Secret*, recommended in
this respect.

65   Fix your attention

On Me.
As immanent in your
Heart,
As Self,
Consciousness,
Godhead,
Source of your being,
Love,
Peace,
Space,
Bliss,
Be in love with That,
Worship That
So you shall reach
That.
I truly promise you
Who are very dear
And special to me.

66 Leaving aside
All spiritual paths
Surrender to me in your Heart
As your sole refuge.
I shall purify you.
Do not over mourn,
For long.

67 This open secret
Of all secrets
You should never tell

To a man or woman
Who is not an earnest
Seeker after truth.
Never to one unwilling
To hear,
Nor to one who speaks
Ill of this teaching.

68   One who with Love
For Me
Immanent in his Heart
Will tell my open secret
To others who love the truth
Will, sooner or later, through Grace,
Come home.

69   No one else
Than Me.
Personified,
As Self,
Consciousness,
Grace,
Space,
Love,
Heart,
Freedom,
Source,
Truth,
Awareness,
Godhead,

"What-Isness"
Does more loving service
To the world
And no one shall be
Dearer to Me
Than he, who is my
Devoted one.

70 One who shall earnestly,
Often read
This divine conversation
As personification of his own Self,
Then worshiping
With the sacrifice of
Seeking for truth
Will please me.
Heartily
This is My conviction!

71 Full of faith,
Empty of ill-will,
Whoever has
Ears to hear
Shall reach
The auspicious place
Of righteous harmony.

72 Did you listen,
Arjuna,
With wholehearted,

One-pointed attention?
Has the hypnotic
Delusion
Of your dark ignorance
Vanished
Like mist before the
Morning sun?

Arjuna replied:

73 Divine hypnosis,
Delusion,
Ignorance,
Are now dispelled,
Oh Krishna.
My true knowledge,
Awareness of Self
As Consciousness,
I have recognized.

74 By Grace
I am free of doubt.
I am now resolved
To fight!

Arjuna has been "enlightened" by Krishna. He now knows he must not resist but wholeheartedly welcome his destiny because it is the will of God or the Source of his own being.

Sanjaya in reporting this conversation to the blind king of the Kurus then says:

75   "Through the power of Rishi Vyasa,
      I have heard his Open Secret
      Of all secrets,
      The True Yoga from the King of Yogas."

Vyasa was the legendary author of the Mahabaratha. Sanjaya's ability to hear all Krishna's dialogue was because Vyasa bestowed the power so he could inform the blind King.

76   Oh, my blind King
      Having heard this
      Divine conversation
      I rejoice! Rejoice!

77   I remember constantly
      That wonderful vision
      Of God.
      Great is my gratitude.
      I rejoice! Rejoice!

78   Wherever Krishna
      Comes
      And Arjuna the Archer
      Appears,
      So will surely follow the beautiful
      Radiant goddesses
      Of Wealth,
      Victory,
      Prosperity,

Eternal Righteous Harmony,
And Enlightenment.
This I know
Beyond any doubt.
I shall ever be grateful
For this beautiful
Song Celestial,
The Bhagavad Gita
Of Lord Krishna.
Thank you.
Pranams.

Epilogue

The great Gita is a cool collyrium
Of sacred truth, divine;
It shall surely heal
The blindness
Caused by the dark ignorance
Of a deluded world.

Appendix 1

Forty-two verses chosen by
Ramana Maharshi (in his order)

Chapter	Verse
II	1
XIII	1
XIII	2
X	20
II	27
II	20
	24
	17
	16

Chapter	Verse
VI	29
IX	22
VII	17
	19
II	55
	71
XII	15
XIV	25
III	17
	18
IV	22
XVIII	61
	62

Appendix 2

Sixty-four most important verses chosen by Ramesh Balsekar

Chapter	Verse
IX	2
	4
X	3
	10
	11
	20
XI	32
	33
XII	12
XIII	22
	23
	29
	30
	31
XVI	5
XVII	3
XVIII	11
	17
	20
	23
	47
	59
	60
	61
	62
	66

Appendix 3

On the Mystic Number Eighteen

Numbers 18, 108, 1008, 10008 are all multiples of nine, which is a mystic number. All multiples of nine added together ultimately become the number nine. This can be verified (16 x 9 = 144; 1 + 4 + 4 = 9).

The mystic number nine is arrived at in this way:

The universe is represented from the three mental a priori factors – time, space, and causation.

The universe is constituted from the three Gunas (Qualities) – Sattva, Rajas, and Tamas.

The universe is controlled by the three functions – creation, preservation, and destruction.

Thus this three times three makes nine a mystic number. It exhausts the definition of the phenomenal universe.

Twice nine or 18 makes the Mahabharata scheme complete.

The 18 portions (Parvas) in the epic define in detail the career of man on earth.

The 18 chapters in the Gita make Yoga philosophy complete.

In Hinduism, verses compared in honor of gods and sages have 108 (an addition of the mystic number 9).

In Western occultism (Pythagorean and Gurdjieffian) we have the Enneagram based on nine. $10 \div 7$ gives a numerical sequence 1, 4, 2, 8, 5, 7. When these are plotted on a circle and the 3, 6, 9 added as a triangle, a beautiful key emerges which can be applied to many situations, including the musical octave. Plotinus synthesized the Platonic Philosophy into Enneads meaning nine.

Appendix 4

Bhagavad Gita Translations Consulted

1. Bhagavad Gitas
   A Selection
   Remesh S Balsekar
   Zen Publications Bombay, 1995

2. Sri Aurobinda
   Sri Aurobinda Divine Life Trust

3. Eknath Easwasan
   Arkana, 1995

4. Arthur Osborne & Prof Kulkarni
   Ramanasraman, 1973

5. Sri Sankaracharya
    Samata Books, Madras, 1977

6. The Song Celestial
    Sir Edwin Arnold
    Routledge & Kegan Paul, 1955

7. S. Radhakrishna
    Mandala, Unwin, 1989

8. The Song of God
    Prabhananda & Isherwood, 1947

9. Swami Chidhavananda
    Sri Ramakrishna, Taporan, 1973

10. Jnaneshwar
    State of New York University New York Press, 1988

11. Juan Mascaro
    Penguin, 1970

12. Albert E. S. Smythe
    Blavatsky Institute, 1937

13. Dilip Kumar Roy
    Hind. New Delhi, 1993

14. W. B. Yeats
    Faber, 1945

Appendix 5

Other Works Consulted

Be As You Are – Teachings of Sri Ramana Maharshi
Edited by David Godman
Arkana, 1985 (Penguin)
The Epics
Ramayana & Mahabharata

Study of Indian History & Culture, 1993
Raja Yoga
Swami Vivekananda
Advaita Ashrama, 1980

The Mahabharata
R. K. Naryan
Mandarin, 1978

Thoughts on the Gita
      Swami Vivekananda
      Advaita Ashrama, 1981

The Final Truth
      Ramesh S. Balsekar
      Advaita Press, 1989

Teachings from The Bhagavad Gita
      H. P. Shastri
      Shanti-Sadan, 1949

Maha-Bharata
      Ramesh Dutt, 1899

System of the Vedanta
      Paul Deussen
      DK Fine Art, Delhi, 1912

Philosophy of the Upanishads
      Paul Deussen
      Dover, 1905

Yoga and Ayurveda
      David Frawley
      Lotus, Wisconsin, 1999

The Gospel of Ramakrishna
      Swami Nikhilananda
      Advaita Ashram, 1949

The Ultimate Understanding
Ramesh S. Balsekar
Watkins Publishing, 2001

Ramana, Shankara and the Forty Verses
Ramana Maharshi & Shankara
Edited by Alan Jacobs
Watkins Publishing, 2001

The Teachers of One
Paula Marvelly
Watkins Publishing, 2001

Appendix 6

Suggestions for further reading

All the following books are available from Watkins Books, 19 Cecil Court, London WC2 4E2
Website: www.watkinsbooks.com

Collected Works of Ramana Maharshi: Be As You Are – Teachings of Ramana Maharshi
> Ed David Godman

A Duet for One, Ashtavakra Gita
> Ramesh S. Balsekar

Avadhuta Gita
> The Chiltern Yoga Trust, 1976

Yoga Vashista
> The Ultimate Understanding
> Ramesh S. Balsekar

Essays on The Gita
> Sri Aurobindo
> Thoughts on the Gita Vivekananda

The Self Aware Universe: How Consciousness Creates the Material World
> Maggie Goswami, Richard E. Reed, Amit
> Goswami, Fred Alan Wood

Fourteen Verses on Raja Yoga[1]
> Swami Sivananda

Raja Yoga
> Vivekananda

---

[1] Sivananda Yoga Centers all over the world offer classes in Raja Yoga, for those who wish to take this preliminary part of teaching from a theoretical to a practical level.